Praise for
Digging In

"Now this is what gardening is really about! It's not only about getting your hands dirty, but it's the experiences and life lessons that grow from the garden. Robert Benson's story is touching, funny, and delightful. I want to see Robert's garden!"

> —REBECCA KOLLS, host of the nationally syndicated *Rebecca's Garden* on NBC and HG-TV, author of the book by the same title, and publisher of *Seasons by Rebecca* magazine

"An enjoyable read for seasoned and beginning gardeners. Robert Benson gives people inspiration."

> —JOHN CARLOFTIS, contributing editor, *Garden Design* magazine

"*Digging In* is a classic of gentle memoir. I will never look at a garden in the same way again, and neither will you. This is Benson at the top of his game."

> —PHYLLIS TICKLE, author of more than two dozen books, including her latest, *The Night Offices,* and The Divine Hours series

"When one is alert to the tenderness of ordinary things—finches and fence posts and fish fries—and when one has a way with words, one is likely to pen books that invite a reader to consider her own ordinary life anew and honor the hidden arts of tending and nurture that gentle our world. Robert Benson does just that in *Digging In.*"

> —WENDY M. WRIGHT, professor of theology, Creighton University, and author of *Seasons of a Family's Life* and *Sacred Dwelling*

"*Digging In* is thoroughly wonderful. Benson's writing is spare, simple, understated, always faintly humorous—and very forceful without seeming to be. As he writes about digging holes for a fence and growing roses, he also uses his spade and shovel to turn over the reader's heart. Before you know it, you are in that garden, invested in its development, and strangely affected by roses you've never seen and a fountain you've never heard. The book delivers what it promises—it digs deep."

—PAULA D'ARCY, speaker and retreat leader and author
of several books, including *Gift of the Red Bird, Sacred
Threshold,* and *Song for Sarah*

"*Charming, unique, poignant, special,* and *dear* describe this remarkable little book. In reading these pages, I feel as though I'm being given permission to look through Robert Benson's window. What I see touches me deeply: love, life, creativity and dreams, growth, humor, hard work, beauty of the earth, blossoms, contemplation, and delight."

—MACRINA WIEDERKEHR, OSB, author of *The Song of the Seed*

"Robert Benson reminds us of what we too often forget—that the ground we walk upon is sacred. With the creative eye of a novelist and the playfulness of a poet, he tutors us in the art of really knowing the place where we live and celebrating the wonders in our own backyards."

—FREDERIC and MARY ANN BRUSSAT, coauthors of *Spiritual
Literacy* and directors of SpiritualityandPractice.com

More Praise for Previous Books by Robert Benson

"Benson's tone remains chatty and down-to-earth, and the analogies he draws hit the mark...."
—*The New York Times Book Review*

"Benson writes mellifluously with original insights and welcome humor.... [He] captures a world in which time slows down and material things become of less importance.... Charming and elegantly written...that rare gift, a thought-provoking record of his own spiritual quest.... Willa Cather's phrase 'Thy will be done in art as it is in heaven' could serve as an epigraph to [his] fine work."
—*Publisher's Weekly*

"The author's language is graceful and his ideas graced...."
—*American Benedictine Review*

"A joy to read...so personal that the reader will feel he knows Robert Benson as an old friend. It is disappointing to awaken from the text and realize otherwise.... The characters and locations...become a meditation and talisman for a deeper existence."
—*Bookpage*

"An eloquent, warmhearted guide to enriching our lives..."
—FORBESBOOKCLUB.COM

"Benson's deceptively sneaky storytelling sneaks up on you. His style...a fusion of gentleness, raw truth, and quiet power."
—NIKKI GRIMES, award-winning author of *Bronx Masquerade*

Digging In

ALSO BY ROBERT BENSON

Digging In

Tending to Life in Your Own Backyard

by Robert Benson

WATERBROOK
PRESS

DIGGING IN
PUBLISHED BY WATERBROOK PRESS
12265 Oracle Boulevard, Suite 200
Colorado Springs, Colorado 80921
A division of Random House Inc.

ISBN 978-1-4000-7173-9

Library of Congress Cataloguing-in-Publication Data
Benson, R. (Robert), 1952-
   Digging in : notes from the back garden / Robert Benson. — 1st ed.
       p. cm.
   Includes bibliographical references.
   ISBN 978-1-4000-7173-9
   1. Gardens—Religious aspects—Christianity. 2. Gardeners—Religious
life. 3. Benson, R. (Robert), 1952- I. Title.
   BV4596.G36B46 2007
   242—dc22

                                                2006100801

Printed in the United States of America
2007—First Edition

10 9 8 7 6 5 4 3 2 1

This book is for JB and Geoffrey,
who brought us to Sunnyside and then
brought us a joy we would
never have known.

———

And it is for Hal,
my friend who taught me what the word
"neighbor" means.

———

And it is for the gardener
who loves me.

And now it is for you, too.

NAMASTE.

R. B.

CONTENTS

With this more substantial shelter about me,
I had made some progress toward settling
in the world.

—HENRY DAVID THOREAU

ONE

Transplanted

To keep the perfect days so that what we have
laboured over and nourished, petted and protected
can be held at its zenith...how badly we would
like to hold it just so.

—MIRABEL OSLER

WE SPENT THE FIRST YEARS of our marriage out in the suburbs about fifteen minutes east of Nashville. But we were not really suburbanites at heart. We like sidewalks and old trees, front porches and old cottages, and restaurants within walking distance.

To the constant curiosity of our suburban neighbors in those days, the two of us did our best to turn our small tract house in an ordinary subdivision into a Victorian cottage, inside and out.

We whitewashed the brick exterior and grew privet hedges around the front edge of the yard and down the sides, trying to grow them tall and unruly and impenetrable to the eyes of people driving by. We put in white board fences and a potting shed and a kitchen garden. We hunkered down behind the hedges and piped opera out the window into the backyard and generally did our best to live as though Rosamunde Pilcher and Miss Jane Marple were just around the corner instead of a Wal-Mart.

One April evening we sat in the yard enjoying a golden sunset, a particular moment we both clearly recall. Surrounded by the first fresh blooms of the lower garden, we were watching the goldfinches come to the feeders. We talked about how good it was going to be to have a summer where we were only maintaining the garden instead of building it, to have a chance to sit and enjoy the season rather than work so hard. We both recall a gentle breeze that evening we thought was the leading edge of a warm front we hoped might bring us a welcome shower. The gentle breeze turned out to be the front edge of the winds of change.

My children were coming.

———

The complete story of how the two of us became the four of us is complicated, and some of it is not even mine to tell.

In those days we saw my two young children on Thursday evenings and every other weekend and at holidays. But a fast-moving and surprising series of circumstances and conversations conspired to produce our invitation for them to come to live with us. It was not something we ever planned on doing, but it seemed the right thing when we did it, and it seems the right thing these years later.

When they said yes, our world changed very quickly.

Within a few days, we put the suburban house on the market and sold it. We started looking for a house large enough to hold us all, in a neighborhood where the children would be zoned to the schools we all agreed were the right ones for them. We found a circa 1910 cottage in an old Victorian-style neighborhood in the heart of the city, a neighborhood called Sunnyside, no less. Ms. Pilcher and Ms. Marple would have been pleased.

Within another month, we were packed up and moved. We had an old house to live in and a new home to make.

———

"The journey through time…is a journey in search," wrote Frederick Buechner. "We search for a self to be. We search for other selves to love. We search for work to do."

Our search for those things often leads us to places we never imagined we would go, places we never imagined we would live. Not very many of us live in the same neighborhood or the same city or the same state we grew up in. The nature of the society in which we live has most of us on the move most of the time—from job to job, town to town, and all too often from relationship to relationship. Being transplanted is something that happens one way or another to most all of us. Putting down new roots is not always an easy thing to do.

The roots from which we came are often buried deeply in soil that we have long since left, or at least most of us have. We go back to visit from time to time—holidays, reunions, weddings, funerals, and other moments in which milestones are marked. The older we get, the truer it is that some of the people who put down the roots from which we grew are gone now. They have joined the crowd of folks "whom we have loved but no longer see," as the old prayer books call them.

We visit our roots, one might say, but the truth is that someone else planted those roots. We grew up, and we went away to find our own futures, make our own homes, and put down our own roots. Wherever we went away to, we are the ones who must do the digging in.

We search for our own selves, for work to call our own, and for others to love. If we are to have any roots at all, we must find them in the places where we are now, on this day. If we are to make a home, if we are to deeply belong to the places in which we find ourselves, we must dig ourselves in somehow. It is in such digging in that we can most tenderly recall the places we came from, most deeply appreciate where we are, and most clearly see who we may yet become. How well we fulfill our dreams and hopes for a place to belong might just come down to how well we tend to the life that is lived in our own backyard. Whether our place is large or small, urban or rural, our first home or our last, a cottage or a condo, these are the places where we must put down roots.

———

Bloom Where You Are Planted was the title of a book I read when I was a teenager. And I later came to laugh at the notion of it, it sounded so sweet and so naive. A lot of things about the sixties were like that. Later still, I finally caught on.

We have no other choice, actually. And so we may as well dig in.

TWO

Please Fence
Me In

My instinct is always

to enclose myself, like a hibernating animal.

—Anne Scott-James

WE FINISHED THE UNLOADING one Saturday night at midnight. The journey from the suburbs to Sunnyside was complete. Or at least the uprooting part was over.

I took a three-hour nap, then got up and tiptoed around the house, moving boxes so we could walk through the halls and get to the refrigerator and find the towels and the silverware.

By noon on Sunday, I was on a plane to Oregon to lead a week-long retreat. The full-time parenting adventure would hit full stride on Monday morning when the time came to get the children ready and off for their first day at the new schools. Cleverly, I was two thousand miles away.

———

"The beginning of wisdom," goes the African proverb, "is to get yourself a roof." But if two teenagers suddenly come to live with you, the beginning of wisdom is to make sure that the roof sits on a two-story house. And that the second story has a three-room suite with a full bath and plenty of closet space so the children have a place they can call their own. While downstairs you get to have a place you can still call your own as well.

We had ourselves a roof, but our new life together, the life the four of us were about to live out every day, had no structure to it yet, no form and no shape—no bones, to use a gardener's term. The shape it had before no longer worked. Our house was home to the children now, not just a place they came to visit. We had to build everything from the ground up. Daily routines and ways of communicating so the small stuff stayed small had to be found. Boundaries had to be set, rituals had to be established, habits had to be formed. There was not much in place the morning I flew off to Oregon.

On Monday evening I called from Portland to see how the first day had gone. "School went fine," came the answer from the ones who had been to school.

"And we got our new kittens," they went on. Though I had known this was going to happen, I was mildly astonished they had waited barely twenty-four hours to add two small, furry beings to what I hoped would be a peaceful abode. I went off to Portland thinking of the pitter-patter of little feet in my hallways at home. And I was coming home to eight more feet than I had said good-bye to. I asked to speak to the person in charge. She caught me up on the day's events from an adult perspective.

"We did have a bit of excitement today in the backyard," I was told.

She had opened the back door to take out the trash. Whereupon she discovered a man she had never seen before with a wheelbarrow full of tools. It shocked her to see him there, even more so when she recognized our wheelbarrow and our tools. In a special voice she uses for such occasions, she asked what he was up to.

He told her he used to live in this house long before it had been rehabbed, and when he walked by and saw the tools, he figured no one wanted them, so he decided to help himself. When she pointed out to him that his explanation made no sense at all to her and would likely make no sense to the police, whose number was being dialed by one of the children even as they spoke, he abandoned the wheelbarrow and vacated the premises with an indignant huff. From the tone of the telephone call, I suspected there was enough indignation in the air to go around.

In those days, Sunnyside was not exactly the Wild West, but it certainly held the potential for more excitement than we had encountered in the suburbs. This once-prosperous middle-class neighborhood fell on hard times as people moved off to college and to the suburbs and other towns.

Now the neighborhood was coming back to life. Though for every cottage being rehabbed, there were a couple of cottages falling down around the ears of an elderly person who no longer could muster the resources or the energy to fix the place up. The neighborhood also contained a couple of dozen badly designed and poorly built duplexes—infill, as they are known—occupied by folks with overgrown yards or yards used as a parking lot for old cars that no longer run.

Scattered through the fifteen square blocks or so we call Sunnyside were six or seven crackhouses, whose crowd of assorted sordid hangers-on roamed the streets and alleyways at all hours of the day and night.

In those days in Sunnyside, the beginning of wisdom was to get yourself a fence.

———

When I flew off to Portland, there was not yet much of a shape to our life together, and the backyard was not in very good shape either.

The backyard was bare and lifeless enough that I flew home from Portland at the end of the week knowing that the leisurely gardening summer we had hoped for had slipped from our grasp and turned into something else altogether. I got a few hours sleep, woke up and put my work boots on, and sat down on the steps to look at the canvas we had to work with. There was not much to look at.

In the first place, the whole yard was pretty small: only twenty steps wide from the stop sign at the corner to the hedge that marks the boundary between our yard and Miss Dessie's, our neighbor. Twenty steps for me equals forty feet. (Golfers know how many feet are in a step; otherwise they do not know which club to use. If you cannot hit it straight, then after the ball sails wide to the right or the left or into the trees, you are able to say, "Well, at least it was the right club." A small victory, but small victories are often what make life bearable.)

The front yard is pocket-size: six steps (twelve feet) from the sidewalk to the porch. From the front edge of the front porch to the backyard is another fifty feet, but almost all of that space is taken up by the house itself. From the back steps of the house to the alley is only thirty-five steps. And that seventy-foot-by-forty-foot space is what we have left in which to put down some roots, of both the literal and figurative varieties.

Along the house on the Miss Dessie side, there is almost no room at all. Two to four feet, and the distance varies depending on the time of year and the thickness of the privet hedge. And either her hedge is crooked or my house is, neither of which would be a surprise. My neighbor Hal says we live in an "eyeball" neighborhood. You work on something for a while trying to get it straight or level, and then you stand back and eyeball it. If it looks right, you declare it level no matter what the instruments say. *On the level* is a relative term, both in Sunnyside and in storytelling.

Sitting on the back steps, you can see that Miss Dessie's hedge runs all the way to the alley. About halfway back toward the right edge of the yard is one glorious maple tree. And running down the left-hand side of the yard is another privet hedge, about fifteen feet high and six feet thick.

When we moved here, the backyard was dirt or mud, depending on the weather, interspersed with scraggly patches of grass. There was one small spot where the sun shone for about six hours a day. Unfortunately, it turned out to be on top of a shelf of rock only about six inches below the surface of the ground.

Just to make it challenging, the yard slides downhill from right to left. The drop is about seven feet altogether.

Between the mud and the weeds, the slope and the rock, the shade and the size, some considerable imagination was required to conjure up a garden worthy of a cottage in a place called Sunnyside. The canvas looked pretty bleak.

With a sigh, I headed off to buy some lumber and some tools. I needed posts for the fence to frame in whatever was going onto this meager canvas. I needed tools to replace the ones stolen by the wheelbarrow man, who had dropped back by in the night, just in case I had forgotten the need for boundaries to be set.

———

There are two ways to go about putting up a fence in one's backyard.

One way is to call someone who builds fences and hire him to come and build one. People who choose this method are likely the sort of people who Google the directions to somewhere rather than learn to read a map. They also can be counted on to stop at a Shell station and ask directions when they are lost. I suspect they inhabit very tidy little houses, get their oil changed regularly, and keep their shoes polished.

I am the other kind of person. So I chose the other fence-acquisition method—I decided to build it myself.

I grew up in a house where the rule was that whenever

technical stuff, like plumbing or electricity, needed to be done, then professional help was acceptable. But if the task merely required sweat and shovels and hammers and nails and saws, then you did it yourself. To hire someone else to do those things was considered a capitulation, a failure to respond to some deep calling. According to my father, *do-it-yourself* was not a marketing slogan for a section in a hardware store; it was a familial imperative.

———

In the suburbs where I grew up in the 1960s, not a great deal of real homesteading work went on. The white-collar world had claimed most of the town by then. My grandfather and my father worked out their remaining pioneer instincts by hammering and digging and sawing and hauling. I know this because I worked beside them whenever school closed down for the day or the weekend or the summer, a member of the cheap, readily available labor force they counted on.

Which brings me to another reason I decided to build the fence myself. I already knew where I could find cheap, readily available labor. They lived upstairs in my house now, and they ate my food, and I drove them to school every day and put clothes on their backs and surrendered an ever-increasing portion of my personal living space to the two kittens they had liberated from the local animal shelter.

Much of what I learned from my father I learned while working in the yard with him. All of the other places where he taught me about being a person and an artist and a husband and a father—I listened to him speak at retreats, I worked with him for years in the family business, I traveled with him for vacation adventures, I sat with him and his friends around countless tables, I talked with him on the telephone about books and sentences and ideas many nights—all of those places were secondary to the time we spent digging in the dirt or hauling a wheelbarrow full of rocks or hammering boards together. Among the other things I learned from him was that people whose work is largely in their heads—publishers and writers and executives and such—do well to learn to do something that makes them sweat.

Other people came to know and love their parents in other ways. I have a friend who says that she fell in love with her dad on Saturdays when they would clean the house and set a grand table for her father's friends, who came each weekend to eat supper and play cards. She would share the dinner and then sit beside the card table on the porch late into the evening, watching and listening and learning what it meant to entertain.

One of our neighbors from up the street went and bought a Harley so he could go riding with his dad. Another took master gardening classes with her mother. One of my golf buddies told me that he played golf with his father almost every weekend when he was growing up. He says, of course, that you can tell more about a person by playing a round of golf with him than by any other method. I say you can tell a fair amount about a person if you put a shovel or hammer in his hands.

I had this notion that building a fence together might well do the same sort of thing for me and my children. And I had a sense that this particular moment in our life together—this time of change and adjustment and adventure—might be exactly the right time.

———

My children had already proved themselves to be good workers when they helped me in the yard on weekends before they came to live with us. I used to hire them to work on Saturday mornings, or bribe them, whichever term you prefer. My theory was they were already going to use my money to buy Legos or to play the snack machines at the YMCA pool in the afternoon, so it might as well end up in their pockets honestly.

So the next week when the lumber arrived and the kids got home from school, I proclaimed the season of the building of the fence. The season turned out to be eighteen months long.

I did not decide we would build the fence ourselves to save time or money. I did it to create memories for myself and my children. And I did it so that from time to time, I could set down my fountain pen and stand in my yard and point to solid evidence of an honest day's work.

———

According to the general contractor, as I like to think of her sometimes, the master plan called for two kinds of fencing.

(She, too, likes the term *general contractor*. The term *master planner* seems to work as well. Other times *empress of quite a lot* will do. I myself am the subcontractor of all trades, master of none at all. The arrangement is clearly the best gig I have ever had.)

One kind of fence, the privacy fence, would satisfy the requirement to block the view into our back garden from the street and alley. The other kind, the open fence, would allow for breezes to come through the yard, maintain a sense of openness to the neighborhood, and keep us from feeling walled in.

Both kinds of fencing would help keep our tools and lawn furniture from sprouting legs and walking off, as Hal likes to say, and eliminate the need for us to keep everything chained to the maple tree. There is something less than congenial about a candlelight dinner in the backyard when everything is tied together with a series of bicycle chains.

We brought a wrought-iron arch from the other house when we moved. It took three of us and a pickup truck to move it. Believing its sheer weight made it safe, we did not chain it to anything. One afternoon I went in the house for a drink of water, and when I came outside about eight minutes later, it had sprouted legs and walked off.

———

The privacy fence was to go along Tenth Avenue from the house to the alley and then up the alley to the hedge separating us from Miss Dessie's. It was to be constructed from eight-foot-by-eight-foot panels of pressure-treated lumber delivered to us ready to hang on four-by-four posts.

The open fence was to be made of one-inch-by-one-inch spindles, hung a few inches apart on two-by-fours connected to the posts. I came across a fence made the same way while walking through the neighborhood one day. When I showed it to the general contractor, she liked it too. She also noticed the top of the spindles had been cut with a small pyramid on the top. We decided to steal that idea as well.

When I got home from the spindle-fence-research-and-approval expedition, I walked everything off—two feet per step, eight feet between the posts, twenty-four spindles per section—and called to order up the spindles and the two-by-fours. During the night I had a nightmare involving sixteen hundred miniature pyramids. The nightmare turned out to be prophetic.

I spent the better part of one afternoon and thirty dollars worth of spindles trying to figure out the geometry necessary to cut spindle pyramids in groups of ten or twelve instead of having to do sixteen hundred of them one at a time. I took a worktable and nailed stops to it to hold the spindles in place and kept trying to figure out how to make one cut and then roll all the spindles over and cut again, and so on, until I had a group of spindles with perfect pyramids on top.

My son came home from school and found me sitting under the maple tree with a cold drink in my hand, a pile of mangled spindles at my feet, and a discouraged look on my face.

"What are you doing?" he asked.

"Wasting lumber," I said.

"Okay, what are you trying to do?"

So I showed him.

He took a pencil and a piece of two-by-four and made a sketch. He made three or four quick measurements. Next he explained some mathematical stuff that included several uses of the word *hypotenuse* and reset the stops on the worktable and picked up the circular saw and whipped out six perfect spindles with perfect pyramids on top. Then he asked for Saturday's work money two days early so he could go to the skate park with some friends. What was I going to say? At least he did not ask for a raise.

———

It turned out my son also had a particular gift for operating an electric drill. When the time came to put the privacy panels up or drill the spindles into the two-by-fours, he was a whiz. Every time we would go to work, he ceremoniously laid out the long lines of extension cords and got his two drills ready—one for drilling the holes and one for setting the screws. He wore a tool belt around his waist with his drills hanging from it like guns in a holster. Then he would sit patiently on a five-gallon paint bucket waiting for his crew—his sister and his father—to haul the boards across the yard, cut them to size, wrestle the crosspieces into place, tap on them to get them level, and hold on to them for dear life while he worked his drill magic. Then he would sit back down.

He was less inclined to be available when it was time to dig the next posthole. Fortunately, I had a daughter. If she had not been such a hard worker, I am reasonably certain I would still be digging postholes by day and guarding my lawn chairs by night.

Most of Middle Tennessee sits on limestone. The rock hides down there under our yards, lurking a foot or so below the surface, waiting for some poor fool to come along and try to dig a hole for a fence post. It had been waiting for me for centuries.

I have seen some hard workers in my day, but I would put my daughter up against anybody in a contest involving the use of a posthole digger. Long arms and legs glistening with sweat, her long blond hair flying out behind her baseball cap, she would attack a spot of ground, claiming it for a posthole, rocks or no rocks.

At one point someone recommended we rent a gas-powered posthole digger. So we did. Working with a gas-powered posthole digger is roughly akin to grabbing a trail bike by its handlebars and trying to get it to stand on its back wheel in one spot while cranking it up to full throttle. Only louder.

We gave up on the heavy equipment after three attempts to dig a decent hole. I will take my daughter and a good old-fashioned tool any day. She did the work faster anyway. And if you are a softball player, as my daughter was at the time, you can build up your forearms while you are at it. This increases your bat speed when the fence building has been completed and batting practice has begun.

The fence building rolled on at its own stately pace. I got up early to do my scribbling, trying to hit my daily word count in the hopes of finishing the book I was working on at the time. In the middle of the day, I went back to work on the fence, doing what I could do alone until one or both of the kids came home from school and could help. The weekends were big for fence building because the school system gave me my crew back for a couple of days.

Things other than writing deadlines and the school system interrupted the work too. One month's fence money would be spent to repair the car or to fix the plumbing. Or the rains would come for a week, and everything would stop. Or I would have to travel to lead a retreat or to do a book show. Then wrestling season came along, and then softball season began. The crew was harder to gather up, and I myself would always rather be somewhere watching my kids play than be in the backyard cutting spindles anyway.

One day a year or so into the fence building, the general contractor announced what could only be considered a completion bond. One could have employed the term *ultimatum,* I suppose. The announcement informed us that the annual trip to the beach for the four of us would not take place this summer until the fence had been completed and the yard and its contents secure.

It turned out that proper incentive was all we ever really needed to muster up the energy to finish the fence. In a few days we were down to the finishing touches. We added some fence alongside the house to form an *allee* to store tools and flowerpots and such. On the Tenth Avenue side, we put in a gate with a big iron bell for neighbors to ring whenever they come to visit. We tied the bell to the gate so it will ring if a not-so-neighborly person comes through the gate to steal a wheelbarrow. We topped off the fence posts with copper caps that shine in the sun.

We had ourselves a fence. It was hardly the Great Wall of China but sturdy enough to keep the wheelbarrow man and his compatriots out and the tools and the lawn furniture in. And besides having a fence, we had a better-than-average pile of memories and a wheelbarrow load of stories to laugh about together. I had taught my children everything I knew about how to act when you cut a board too short, hit your thumb with a hammer, and put the post-hole in the wrong place. They had taught me about who they were and who they were becoming and how I might be of help along the way. My father was right; you do learn a lot about people if you put a hammer in their hands.

Now we had some boundaries, and we could see the edges of the canvas.

We were at the beach for a vacation. The telephone rang, and it was Hal. He was watching our house for us while we were away—picking up the mail and feeding the cats and doing other good neighbor sorts of things. He asked if we had our computer with us. We did, and so we hung up the phone and opened up the e-mail to see the photos he said would be there.

Someone in a car had run through the stop sign at the corner by our house and plowed into another car going down Tenth. The photographs showed that a car sat tucked in under our bedroom window. Under the car I could just make out the remains of the front gate and two shattered fence posts. The other four or five sections of the fence leaned back on one another, folded up like a fan.

Three of the photos featured our neighbors. In Sunnyside, any excuse to stand around and visit will do. A wreck, even a small one, typically brings all of us out to stand around and talk and watch other people work.

We called Hal back, and he had already done the stuff good neighbors do. He had gotten a copy of the police report and called the insurance man and given him the photos. Since whoever wanted to could now walk into the yard and take anything they wanted, he had moved the most vulnerable things to his yard for safekeeping and chained up the rest. When you choose a neighborhood, choose one that has a Hal in it.

When we got home, I called someone to come and repair the fence. I do not know if I was too busy or if I simply could not bear the thought of working on it anymore.

The fence company sent out Bill and Harold, two men who had been putting up fences for a living for about forty years.

They began the repair work with an extended period of standing around and smoking. They made a lot of the same noises mechanics make in those moments before they tell you that what needs to be done next will cost a lot of money and could have been avoided if only you had been smart enough to call them in sooner and were not so inept in general. After a lifetime of owning mechanical things that rarely work the way they are supposed to, I am very familiar with such noises and what they mean.

I got ready to be "dadded" in a serious way.

You are being dadded when someone who is considered an expert watches you do the work that they know how to do. As they watch, they tell you why the way you are doing it will not actually work. They unfailingly wait for the task to be about half-finished before they tell you this, and they do so with a bemused look on their faces. One can be dadded retroactively too, when something fails.

There is a corollary known as being "mommed"—the term means essentially the same thing only it comes from someone who has never actually done the work before, has no intention of ever actually doing the work, and possibly has not ever even watched the work being done before.

(I hasten to add that I am not responsible for the gender bias implied in these two terms. My experience tells me either sex is capable of operating from either position. I did not coin these terms; I am only reporting out.)

Harold cleared his throat, and Bill lit another cigarette, and I steeled myself for the retroactive dadding to come.

Harold turned to Bill. "That's some fence, ain't it?"

"Who built it anyway?" asked Bill as he turned to look at me.

"We did it ourselves. Me and my kids." They looked at each other. Now Bill cleared his throat, and Harold lit a cigarette.

While I was waiting for judgment to be passed, I thought of the three of us out there working all those afternoons. I thought of how we laughed and sweated together. I thought of those days when we had no boundaries or rituals, the days when we had no fence either. I was about to see if any of it would pass muster.

"The whole thing woulda come down if you hadn't built it so strong," Harold said. "That's one fine fence."

Well, it is a start, I thought. If we can muddle along together and make this one thing strong, perhaps we can summon up what it takes to make strong some of the other parts of our new life together as well.

THREE

Pop Tests and Wally Dirt

There is no such thing

as a life that does not return.

—John le Carré

I KNOW TWO THINGS TO BE TRUE about working in the garden. The first is that it helps to have the right tool, and it does not hurt to know how to use it. My grandfather Pop taught me that.

Wally was my other grandfather, and he taught me the other true thing: all dirt is not created equal. There is good dirt, and there is bad dirt. And then there is Wally dirt.

Wally dirt is what we have at our house.

Pop was my father's father. His name was John Thomas Benson, but his grandchildren called him Pop. So did nearly everyone else, including my grandmother. John was the name she used when she was unhappy with him.

I remember his coming to visit us in Florida when I

was very young, pulling his silver Airstream trailer into the back lot behind the church my father pastored.

We, in turn, visited him in Nashville. I remember riding all night from Orlando in the backseat of my father's Ford Galaxie to be at Pop's in time for Christmas. Here stood a great stone house that rambled across a great piece of land. It seemed like a grand estate to a four-year-old boy who lived in three rooms in the back of a breeze-block church in Orlando. Years later Pop sold that place and bought fourteen acres along the old main channel of the Cumberland River, thirty miles north of Nashville.

My father had moved us all back to Tennessee by then, and he bought four of the acres from Pop to build a house on.

The land was almost completely covered in woods when Pop bought it. You could stand about forty yards from the river and not even be able to see the water. We had to clear the land before anyone could build on it.

I say *we* cleared it. I was only seven or eight years old when the work began. I mean Pop and my father and my younger brother and myself. And James Hackney, a large African American man who worked for my grandfather a few days a week.

Many a Saturday morning and on Sundays after church, my brother and my father and I would pile into the car and drive the twenty miles or so north to "the property," as my grandfather taught us to call it.

We would leave the four-lane highway at Indian Lake Road and travel five miles down a gravel road, through the fields and down the hill between the two ponds, around the curve by Mr. Barr's house, up the steep hill that later became the center of the sledding world, and around the next curve to the property.

My grandfather and James would be under the big oak tree in the center of the property. There would be boxes of doughnuts and bottles of Coke, with cheese and crackers and Vienna sausages for lunch. We would change our clothes in the car—and change from little boys into lumberjacks.

Once the land was cleared and the houses were built, I pretty much saw Pop every day of my life on that land until I moved out on my own. If I did not see him, then I heard him. I could hear his tractor going or one of his chain saws. I could hear him calling out to James or one of the other men who worked for him. I could hear him sneeze from time to time; the sound of Pop sneezing was sort of a legend. No one ever sneezed with more gusto than he did. They say that when you sneeze, you are as close to death as you ever are and yet still remain alive. He would celebrate a sneeze with a loud *whew!* at the end. Which proved to me that Pop believed in resurrection enough to celebrate it every time he got a chance.

Until I went away to college, many of my afternoons and some portion of my weekends were spent working in the yard, either over by Pop's house or by ours. During the land-clearing years, it was mostly cutting trees and hauling stuff to the burn pile and putting chains on logs and dragging them away with a tractor. Once we all moved into the houses, there were split-rail fences to build and gardens to till and endless grass to mow. There was a rock wall to build along the shoreline so the riverbank would not erode and trees to plant and drainage ditches to dig. I majored in English in college since I already had earned a minor in landscaping and general labor.

Those were the days I learned about tractors and chain saws and axes. I learned how to lay a brick patio and how to break rock and how to cut boards. I learned how to mix concrete and how to plant a tree and how to build a fire.

I did not master everything, of course. Pop had a way of testing you—to see if you could hook a chain to a log properly or bank a fire just right—that could make you start to sweat just knowing that he was going to ask you to do it. He tried to teach me about fishing poles and shotguns too, and I washed out in both cases, much to his chagrin.

But I did learn to love the feel of the tools in my hands and to love the work itself. Those were the days when I was learning what it means to dig in, I think. I may yet pass that test.

———

But I learned about dirt at Wally's house.

Wally was my mother's father, and he lived in an old neighborhood in Nashville in a small brick house on a proper-sized neighborhood lot. Nobody ever called it "the property."

He actually had two lots. The house was on one, and the other became his side yard. The side yard had big open spaces where baseball and touch football and croquet could be played, if you were careful about the fountain and the flower beds. He had roses and other things, but mostly he had irises. The irises were forever being divided, and Wally's iris bulbs bloom each spring all over town. Everyone who ever knew him or my mother or her sister has some. Including me.

Along the back fence at Wally's house, there was a privet hedge that got loose from its owners and was taking over Wally's backyard. Several good-sized old trees were back there too and a path that wound its way through the trees and the hedge. The path had nowhere much to go; the space it was wandering through was only about a thousand square feet altogether. But for a certain ten-year-old boy on certain afternoons when he was growing up, the whole world lived back there in that little thicket.

The Hardy boys lived there and Nancy Drew and most of the Indians of the Wild West. You could climb the old maple tree by the house and look out over King Arthur's realm, and you could see pirates coming from the beach to attack the fort. Up under those hedges and trees a young boy could hunt bears and rescue maidens and explore caves and change the outcome of the battle of

Gettysburg. He could ride a horse along those paths and rescue the defenders of the Alamo. The same paths would sneak him into France just before D day to mark the landing zones for the paratroopers.

Even now if the boy closes his eyes, he can see those trees and hedges, and he can smell the dirt—Wally dirt.

———

Not only was Wally's yard very different from Pop's, so was his life.

Pop started out his working life as a printing salesman. His father had started a printing business in Nashville before the turn of the last century, a highly successful business at that. Pop's older brothers took up their places in the family business before Pop was even born. When the time came, Pop went to work, traveling from town to town landing contracts to print yearbooks, the core of the family business. At one time, the company printed nearly a quarter of the nation's college yearbooks.

My great-grandfather had also started a small music publishing company that produced songbooks for churches. After he passed away, the music publishing sort of languished until Pop came along.

One day he told his brothers someone wanted to buy the publishing business. They said it was okay with them and signed the papers. Pop wrote them a check and went down the hall as the owner of his own publishing company. He had been saving his printing commissions for months until he had enough money to meet the price he had set. Before all was said and done, the publishing company grew to become the second largest holder of religious music copyrights in the world.

Wally, on the other hand, was a bookkeeper by trade. He worked in several cities in the South when he was young, bookkeeping his way through North Carolina and Virginia and Georgia. Finally he came back to Nashville, his hometown, and stayed here the rest of his life.

The first time that I ever went to see him at his office,

I walked the few blocks from the big building where the Benson family offices were to a little building on the corner of Eighth Avenue and Church Street and went up to the third floor, and there he was. It was only a few blocks, but it might as well have been a continent away.

Wally was not much of a businessman. Not in practice and certainly not in his heart. In his heart, he was a classical pianist. He dreamed of pursuing a career as a pianist, but his father would not hear of it. So Wally learned a trade that was useful to businesspeople and spent a large portion of his life selling his life by the hour so that someone else could be a successful businessman.

Wally lived for Sundays, when he would play the organ and lead the little choir at church. He never stuck with any of his bookkeeping jobs for very long, but he stayed on as the organist at Memorial Lutheran Church on Riverside Drive in East Nashville for forty years.

Pop's life was built around always building some big thing—a publishing business, a big house out on Brush

Hill Road to raise his family in, an even bigger house out north of town when they had long been gone.

Wally, on the other hand, lived the majority of his adult life in the same little house in the same little neighborhood on the same little patch of ground.

Pop was a builder; Wally was a gardener. Pop had property; Wally had irises.

I learned about tools from Pop. I learned about digging in from Wally.

———

Two blocks south of our corner is a park. There is an eighteenth-century mansion on the top of the hill in the park. The mansion is called Sunnyside, hence the name for our neighborhood.

The land the neighborhood sits on was once farm- and pastureland. Early in the twentieth century, the land was sold off, and trolley-car neighborhoods were built. One trolley-car line came right out Tenth Avenue, past the corner where our house is. Most of the houses in our neighborhood were built between 1905 and 1920. It is hard to know for sure, because a fire at the courthouse destroyed many of the records.

Most of the houses are small, frame houses, cottages really, with front porches and small lots and old trees that were planted when the houses were first built. It is a sidewalk neighborhood, where people actually walk on the sidewalks and say hello to their neighbors on the way to the bus stop or to get coffee or to pick up the papers or to go and play in the park around Sunnyside.

In newer neighborhoods in our city, the developers came in with bulldozers and scraped all the topsoil off to make the place level before construction began. That is not what happened in Sunnyside.

Our houses were planted on the topsoil. Over the years, the soil just got richer. Season after season of leaves from old trees and decades of coal and brick dust have turned the dirt in Sunnyside into fertile black soil just waiting for you to plant something in it and stand back. You dig down into it and hold the dirt in your hand, and it smells good and rich and alive.

Green-thumb folks talk about gardeners who are so good that they can root a Popsicle stick. I do not know if such a thing is possible, but if a Popsicle stick is going to take root anywhere at all, it will be in dirt like the dirt in our yard.

A few weeks after we moved in, on the first weekend we started yard work, I sat down under the maple tree to rest. I had been working for a good while, and I had dirt all over me from digging. We had taken a day off from putting in fence posts so we could plant iris bulbs. They were a housewarming gift from my aunt; they came from Wally's house.

Something seemed familiar to me, something I could not name. I found myself thinking about all those days I had spent working on the property when I was growing up. I was thinking about Pop and James and my brother and my dad, about the tools and the tests and the trees and the tractors. I was thinking, too, about having this little place of my own to dig into, and I was glad not to need a tractor.

Looking at the iris bulbs got me to thinking about Wally's house too and the hours I had spent playing in his backyard. It took a little while for me to figure out what it was that seemed so familiar to me, sitting under our maple, but I finally did. I realized we were planting Wally irises in what could only be described as Wally dirt.

If I was not at home in some way, it sure smelled like home.

When we started looking for houses, we almost bought another one instead. My mother was silently rooting for us to choose this one all along.

She lived in a town house just on the other side of the park, and she was hoping for us to live close by. But she had another reason for liking this house, one that she had been silent about while we were making up our minds.

She came by one afternoon after we had moved in and had begun to work in the yard. "Come on," she said. "I want to show you something."

She led me up the sidewalk along Tenth to where another little yellow cottage like ours sits with a maple tree in the backyard. She sat down on the steps and patted the top of them so that I would sit down beside her.

"I used to sit on these very steps in the afternoons after school and wait for my father to come home on the trolley car," she said. I did not know that Wally had ever lived in this neighborhood.

She went on to tell me that this little house was where they lived for a couple of years when they first moved back to Nashville from Atlanta. She went to school in the old building just up the street and rode her bike to the store a couple of blocks farther on. She was in that store picking up something for her mother when she heard the news that Franklin Roosevelt had died, she told me, and she had left her bike and run all the way home in tears to tell her mother.

"No kidding," I said.

She told me some other stories about Wally that day. He used to keep the books for a bakery three blocks from my house, and she used to walk him to work sometimes. There were other stories, but I barely heard, I confess; I was listening to my imagination, hearing trolley cars and Wally's voice and his footsteps and the sound of a piano in the other room.

"Your grandfather used to walk these sidewalks," she said. "We planted irises in the dirt in this neighborhood long before you did. He shared them with everyone back then too."

We walked back down the street.

"I did not want to tell you these stories before you decided which house to buy." Then she took my hand.

"But I am glad you chose the one you chose. Wally would have been glad too."

———

I grew up thinking that perhaps I was going to be like Pop and my dad—a successful businessman, a big pile of kids, a big house somewhere on a lot of acres. I figured my life would take on the same sort of shape as had all the Bensons before me.

It has not turned out that way at all. I was never much of a businessman, though I tried for a while. And in the end, I have landed in a small house in an old neighborhood with a maple tree and an unruly privet hedge that has gotten away from one of my neighbors. I am more Wally than it ever occurred to me I might be.

And I am not unhappy. In fact, I am more happy more often than I ever could have imagined, or did imagine, during all those years when I was clearing trees on the property alongside Pop or playing in the tiny thicket behind Wally's house. I have a place of my own, a place where I can break out the tools and dig in the dirt. A place that I can help shape and tend, a place where some memories can be made, memories that may yet be held dear by someone long after I have returned to dust. Memories that will be a part of who they become.

After all this time, I have gone from playing in Wally dirt to living on it in a way. Every time I walk these sidewalks and sit on a neighbor's porch under the shade of one of these old trees, I am walking and sitting where Wally did. I am digging in here, and it feels like home. Especially on the days when the suspiciously familiar irises are in bloom here in Sunnyside.

FOUR

Rose Hips and Rose Knees

After such a day my fingers

are bleeding, knees tottering,

back bent, dress muddy and soaking

and shoes an offence...

but I have attained

the most profound inward peace.

—ANNA LEA MERRITT

WHEN THE FENCE WAS IN and the boundaries were set and the tools were safe, the updated master plan was revealed. It called for flower beds here and there and everywhere, so I exchanged my work boots for garden clogs, my hammer for a shovel, and my saw for a mattock and headed out to the back garden.

As is my way, the work began with a brief sit-down under the maple, better to contemplate the impending joys of summer days with less and less grass to mow.

———

The two of us—the general contractor and I—agree that one cannot have too many flower beds. We have the same point of view for completely different reasons.

She maintains that the more flower beds you have, the

more flowers you can actually plant. A logical conclusion for someone who loves flowers as much as she does and believes that having flowers is the reason for having beds to put them in.

My perspective is different. I love flowers, but I do not really consider myself a flower person. My personal experience is that flowers and the beds you put them in come with a host of aggravations. Weeding, deadheading, edging, and mulching, to name a few. In the pitifully small spaces of time in between doing those things, you must dig up a plant and move it to a more "congenial spot"—a gardener's term whose essential meaning is "I put it in the wrong spot to begin with, but I am not about to admit it to the one who has to dig it up and move it." Some plants must be divided from time to time, and therefore some flower beds must be expanded from time to time, both of which create opportunities for digging additional holes and for bonus weeding and edging and mulching.

The one clear advantage in having flower beds, from

my perspective as the subcontractor in charge of weeding, edging, and mulching, is that flower beds eliminate lawn. I will not go so far as to say I believe the only good lawn is a dead lawn, but I do believe a lawn should always be receding, going farther and farther back, like a tide going out never to return. Large expanses of grass should be confined to golf courses and baseball diamonds, where God intended them to be in the first place. There they can be attended to by armies of groundskeepers on little tractors the way they should be.

———

I have considerable experience with lawns and lawn elimination.

My younger brother and I were largely responsible for mowing the grass on the four acres by the river from the time I was about twelve years old. We took turns driving the tractor—not your little suburban lawn tractor, but a Cub Lo-Boy just like Pop's, no less. We also spent a lot of hours doing the trim work, using one of a series of push mowers we managed to kill off in various and sundry ways over the years.

My father liked to spend his weekends piddling in the yard, as he called it. Piddling meant building fences or bricking in patios or planting trees or knocking together porches. Any time spent mowing the grass on the weekend took away from his piddling time. So the deal was that my brother and I mowed the grass by Friday evening before Dad came flying down the driveway ready to begin the piddling for the weekend. Otherwise, instead of being rousted out early on Saturday morning to form up as the piddler's labor force, we had to get up before the piddler did and finish the mowing before we got to form up as the labor force.

My memory may be skewed somewhat—years of riding a tractor can be hard on the little gray cells—but I believe I spent more of my teenage hours mowing grass than I spent on any other activity. When I think of my youth, I think of long, hot, dusty summer afternoons sitting on the tractor. I have been dedicated to the principle of lawn elimination ever since.

I do not actually think of myself as a gardener; *yard worker* is the more proper term. I could be a dirt farmer, since dirt is the one thing I seem to be able to grow.

But I live with a real gardener. Early in our marriage, when we lived in the house she owned in the suburbs, it became pretty clear pretty quickly that if I wanted to spend Saturdays with her, and I did and I do, then I would have to be out in the yard working with her in the garden. Having the lawn mowed by Friday afternoon guaranteed I could spend the weekend piddling in the yard next to her. It was a trade I was, and still am, happy to make.

Before I came along, she had always had more ideas for flower beds in her yard than she had either the time or the labor force to put in. Then I came along. Unbeknownst to her, I had long been dedicated to the global struggle to eliminate lawn.

In the first two years alone, she got a kitchen garden, a toolshed, a hydrangea garden, a fence around the kitchen garden, a hosta garden, and three long flower beds for cut flowers. It thrilled her to think she had married a gardener and to have all these places to plant things. It thrilled me to have eliminated about half the lawn in a relatively short period of time.

So when the call went out for flower beds in our corner of Sunnyside, I put a grin on my face and sallied forth to open up a second front in the eternal struggle.

When we first moved in, scraggly grass and weeds and mud notwithstanding, it took just under two hours to mow and trim the Sunnyside lawn. That included the time spent walking up the street to borrow from and then return the gas-powered mower to John and Wendy. I learned over the years that if the mower gods think I am the owner of the mower that is about to be used, the mower will not start about two-thirds of the time. I also learned that my neighbor's mower always starts, so I borrow it.

The Sunnyside lawn-elimination project has reached the point where I can mow the grass in fifteen minutes. I even use one of those new versions of the classic reel mowers. It makes this gentle whirring sound when I push it instead of a huge roar. It does not throw dust and grass clippings into the flower beds. Best of all, it starts every time. If I can walk, then the mower runs.

There was not much growing in our yard when we got here. The young man who rehabbed the house before we bought it put in just enough landscaping to make it inviting enough for someone to take the place off his hands— monkey grass along the sidewalk leading to the house, a pair of rhododendrons beside the steps, and a few red-tipped photinias under the front windows.

The best thing he did was put a split birch tree in the corner of the front yard. We love the way its silvery leaves flitter and twinkle in the breeze and the sun.

He put a For Sale sign in the front yard, pronounced it ready to be sold, and evidently assumed the new owners would be happy to mow the backyard for the rest of their lives. He obviously had never met a real flower gardener or a committed lawn eliminator.

———

The gardener who lives at our house maintains that roses come first. And so they did.

The roses in our yard came from Texas and Oregon. We found two nurseries that specialize in cultivating Old English roses—great, hardy, rambling roses perfectly suited to growing on spindled fences in the wilds of post-Victorian Sunnyside. The gardener spent the better part of the winter looking through rose books and catalogs, drawing sketches, and plotting combinations of colors. Then we spent a couple of afternoons walking back and forth across the small patch of ground between the front gate and the back corner of the house, the only space with enough sun to grow roses. Using garden hoses to outline the shapes of the beds, we ended up with a meandering walkway that opens into a small circle that leads into the back garden. Once the beds were laid out, she went in the house to check her charts and order up the roses, and I went for my tools.

I worked off and on, piddling away, from late winter into early spring, cutting the beds in. The roses were due to arrive in early April, and the beds had to be ready.

Winters being not particularly cold here, I spent a lot of afternoons between Thanksgiving and April Fools' Day on my hands and knees, taking up turf in two-square-foot patches. About halfway through the project, I watched a gardening show for the first time in my yard-working life and learned you could rent a gas-powered machine to cut up the turf for you. But I passed on it. The lesson I learned with the posthole digger was still fresh in my memory. Besides, when you use big, noisy machines to do your digging, you chase the robins away.

It seems to be true that if you want to see robins come bob, bob, bobbing along in your direction, all you need to do is dig up a pile of dirt. They love it when you do; it makes it easier for them to locate worms. There are robins in this neighborhood who still look back on those turf-removal days with a nostalgic glow in their little hearts for the way I fed them one winter. Some of them still bob their little heads and say, "Thank you, sir," when they see me coming. Generations of robins in Sunnyside call me blessed.

I hauled the patches of turf out to the back, where I piled them up to level off the space between the back fence and the alley. (Not only did I learn how to mow grass during my youth, I also had multiple opportunities for learning that garbage cans seem to work better when they have a level place to stand.) I had a compost pile working back there too, because I knew I would need fill dirt later on in the spring.

Gradually the rose beds took shape. With hope in our

hearts, we added some trellises along the house so roses could someday climb up toward the windows. I built some short pieces of spindle fence to hold the roses that would grow to hide the air conditioner units from view.

One day we saw an ad in the paper for a shop selling wrought iron that originally had been in a park in Cairo and then removed when Cairo officials decided to renew the urban there. During the years the British occupied Egypt, they sent designers and craftsmen and raw materials to Egypt to make proper decorative pieces for their houses and parks and gardens.

My limited experience—we only bought six pieces—suggests one can find no heavier objects on the face of the planet. One does not carry these bits of fence; one drags them across the yard, stopping every few feet to rest one's arms and mutter under one's breath and check one's heart rate. I wrestled two of them into place in the rose garden—long, curved pieces that fit perfectly into the curves of the beds to gently guide one along the path to the back garden.

I came home from running an errand one day in early April. The rose gardener met me at the front door with her charts under her arm and her clogs on her feet and a grin across her face and excitement in her voice.

"They are here, they are here. And they are in the backyard waiting for us."

"Who is here?"

"The roses, the roses—come and meet them."

And then she fairly danced down the hall and out the back door. And I followed.

———

The first batch of our new friends from the nurseries in Oregon and Texas had arrived. Pulled from their boxes, they sat in rows along a large worktable, a troop of plastic pots of roses, most of them no more than six to eight inches tall. They looked too small for such a long journey.

The rose gardener made the introductions.

Cecile Brunner was on the front row, one of our

favorites. She would grow to be tall someday. We had one before at our house in the suburbs, and she took over a plum tree, and we used to see blooms forty feet up in the air. I knew her well enough to know that in a few springs I would have to tie her to the roof to keep her back far enough so I could still get the front gate open.

There was New Dawn, who is not really an old rose; she just looks like one. She would bloom white and sparkling someday, over and over in summer. She would wrap her way through and then up and around the spindles and over the top of the fence. When the breeze was right, she would look for all the world like a gentle wave breaking white in the sun.

Madame Hardy was there. Her canes would be almost as thick as my wrist someday, and she would climb up to peek in the gardener's window and watch over her as she works and receive a happy grin in return whenever a new blossom breaks open.

I met Empress Josephine for the first time that day. Our

hope was to train her as a ground cover along the two-foot slope between the fence and the sidewalk. She would steadfastly resist all attempts to force her to do so. Not unexpected behavior from an empress, to be sure.

Granny Grimmetts, a new friend to me, was there too; her rich blooms would be beautiful to look at, but it would be her scent that would make us swoon on certain summer days.

They would all be beautiful to behold someday. But on that first day, as I looked at them standing in rows with their handwritten identification tags, they looked like refugees— tiny and fragile and helpless and completely incapable of filling all these beds I had dug. For a brief moment, I sat down in the circle in the center of the rose garden and wondered if overelimination of lawn was possible.

My moment of doubt was swept away by the unrolling of the charts and sketches along the worktable. The rose gardener had started putting down clay pots to mark the places where holes were to be dug. Twenty-four inches square and thirty-six inches deep gave enough room for the rose and the planting mixture and the few trowels of dirt they grew up in and brought with them from the West. After I dug the holes, the rose gardener came along and put the plants in their new home.

That is when the murmuring began.

"You are going to love it here," she said to them as she patted them into their new digs. "This is Wally dirt, the best dirt in the world, and you are going to love it here."

"Wait until you climb the fence and the neighbors can see you," she whispered to some of them as she watered them in. "Wait until they see you when they come down the sidewalk."

"You are going to be famous here in Sunnyside," she told them as she pushed dirt up around their tiny selves.

———

She was right; they are among the most famous flower beds in Sunnyside. But they are not alone.

The shade beds up the street at Kim's house have grown lush and cool now. Todd's crepe myrtles tower over his fence with a noble grace.

The bulbs June planted along the sidewalk tell us spring is here. In April, Mr. Burke's dogwood can be so pretty it almost brings me to tears every year. Lela's hydrangeas and Joan's sunflowers announce the summer.

For a few weeks each summer, I have to go by Marilyn's house. She planted the whole front yard in native wildflowers, and when they are in bloom, her yard is a great and glorious mass of flowers. I check the geraniums on the porch of Miss Ruth's house on my way home. And I walk the streets and wonder how many of the neighborhood's irises belonged to Wally at one time.

My gardening expertise has some limits, but I do know this much: any patch of dirt, no matter how large or how small, if tended a little bit, holds within it the possibility of enough beauty to take your breath away. It can grow something that will catch your eye and touch your heart. It can give you something to look forward to when the days are dark and cold.

Real gardeners have always known this. I learned it by being lucky enough to plant myself next to one and by mowing the grass on Fridays so I could piddle in the yard next to her on Saturdays.

———

Right toward the end of the month of the rose planting—a few arrived each week, forty-five in all—my knees began to hurt. I played basketball in high school and college, and for years after that I played pickup games at the YMCA. My knees troubled me all along, and they finally hurt so badly I had to give up playing basketball. The game clearly had passed me by anyway, and I was getting my hat handed to me by younger and stronger guys every time I took the court. I took up golf and have begun to eliminate lawn during my leisure hours, one divot at a time.

The Monday after I spent the weekend digging the

holes for the last of the roses, one of my knees hurt so much I could not walk. Two days later my doctor sent me to a sports-medicine clinic, where they poked and prodded and took x-rays and parked me in a room filled with autographed pictures of the world-class athletes they had treated. Then the orthopedic surgeon came in to talk to me about the pictures of the inside of my knee.

"We have to go in there," he said, pointing at my kneecap. "We need to scrape some stuff off here and here and here," he said as he pointed to closeups of parts of my knee I did not even know existed. "We will have you back out there competing again in no time."

He looked at me expectantly. I think he thought I was going to tell him that I could hardly wait to get back to running marathons or playing pickup ball somewhere or that I hurt myself setting a personal best in a triathlon. I have no research to back this up, but I suspect rose gardening would not likely be considered a contact sport by a guy who spends most of his days performing surgery on power forwards and fullbacks and goalies.

I could not find it within me to tell him I blew out my knee planting roses. I briefly considered telling him about my role as the assistant girls' softball coach for a high school, but I feared additional conversation might shed light on the fact that I mostly kept the score book and hit fungoes. Both of which are fun to me and important to a softball team but neither of which would likely be impressive to an orthopedic surgeon in a sports-medicine clinic. So I just said, "That's great. I'll be glad to get back out there."

At the time we said our vows, my rose gardener married me for better or for worse, but she did not know I was going to fall apart quite so soon. To have and to hold until my meniscus did part. In sickness and in health, and for a few weeks on a cane.

Because of the knee surgery, I missed the opening few days of the softball season that year. The roses were worth it.

There are mornings in the late spring now when we sit in the rose garden with the sun coming up and the dew beginning to fade, and the roses are in bloom, and we sip our coffee gratefully and fully believe no finer three-hundred-square-foot patch of earth can be found anywhere at all.

There are late afternoons too, when we are tired and worn, and we can lie on our backs in the shade and look up to see ourselves surrounded by pink and white and red roses ten and twelve feet above us. Neighbors will walk by on the sidewalk six feet away, and the roses are so thick they cannot even see us.

"Oh, honey, the roses," one of them will say as they go by. Sometimes our giggles give us away.

There are nights when we sit at the table under the maple tree, and the breeze brings the scent of the roses across the yard to us, and it will stop whatever conversation we are trying to make, rendering talk suddenly unnecessary altogether.

All in all, trading a few yards of scraggly grass for such beauty and for such moments is one of the better trades I ever made. If I had to do it over again, I would throw in the other knee if that is what it took to close the deal.

FIVE

Waiting Room

If I were asked to name the chief benefit
of the house, I should say:
the house shelters daydreaming,
the house protects the dreamer,
the house allows one to dream in peace.

—Gaston Bachelard

DEDICATING A ROOM IN A SMALL HOUSE to the writerly activities of the writer who lives here was never really a possibility. After a brief consideration of putting a dungeon in the basement, the decision was made to build a room for him in the corner of the backyard. Given what I had already learned out back about hard work and growing things and starting over and digging through the dirt, it seemed only natural to move the writer to the garden. Downright organic even.

It was always properly assumed that the writer's room needed to be as far from the normal human activity of normal human beings as possible. The constant muttering and the occasional scream emanating from such a place can be disconcerting, especially when another member of the household may be trying to sleep or talk on the telephone or entertain polite company.

And it called for a place where the writer could leave his stuff spread out in piles and allow some piles to go untouched for months. It had to have one table to write on when it was time to use his fountain pen and another table for when he used a computer. There had to be enough bookcases to hold dozens of books and still have shelf space left over for collecting bits and pieces of stuff—baseballs and shells and cards and photos—the things he must hold on to in order to remind him of the real world he lives in whenever he leaves the writing room for the day.

The room had to be just large enough for the writer to pace in a small circle but not large enough for him to live in, because the people back home, on the other side of the garden, would miss him if he did not come home.

I had waited for this moment for years. When I was growing up and dreaming of being a writer someday—a daydream I often dreamed while mowing the grass—I had always seen myself in some distant day going off to a little room to write. In my dream it was a little rose-covered cottage, though I do not know exactly why. It may be that I lived for too long under the influence of too many romantic poets.

I put my boots on and sat down under the maple tree and contemplated what the little building might be like now that it was about to be at all.

———

Of course, I wanted to build it myself. After all of those years of banging on things with my father, I had a notion it would be great fun to actually build something from the ground up. I had once been a weekend member of an informal construction crew, and we raised a three-room farmhouse for my sister. A ten-by-ten building seemed within my capabilities. I would have been given a chance to build the writer's room myself had not two things occurred.

The first was a conversation with the master gardener

in which words like *weatherproof, sturdy, safe,* and *handsome* were mentioned an excessive number of times. Later in the same conversation, the word *timely* came up. There were not a few references to how long it took to raise the fence, references I still consider as hitting below the tool belt. The conversation took place while we sat under the maple tree in the backyard looking through the hedge to where my neighbor's poorly built, unfinished, and therefore shabby outbuilding stood in plain view, providing a decaying, unpainted, and silent exclamation point.

The second blow to my dream of building the place myself came in the form of an unexpected royalty check from a publisher. Some would call it a windfall, but I have been standing in the wind for years both before and after, and it is rare for a breeze to bring a check. I prefer the word *earnings.*

The check was large enough that the master gardener thought we might be able to have the thing built by carpenters who knew what they were doing. She was right, of course. However, once it was up, I could take my tools and do anything I wanted to as long as it was on the inside. The writer would have a place, and might even have it while still young enough to walk to it without a cane.

The master planner then began to do what master planners do: she got on the telephone. After a day or two of asking questions and getting estimates, we got in the car and made a field trip north of the city. We were headed to talk to a company that builds tack rooms for people with horses and storage sheds for people's lawn-care equipment.

I worried a bit on the way that a man who built places to store saddles and hide Weed Eaters would not be up to the task of building a proper room for a poet.

We spent a couple of hours walking in and out of their buildings and looking at plans and price lists and talking through the modifications and additions we could make within the confines of the budget. Most tack rooms do not have covered porches and french doors. They showed us notebooks full of color brochures and floor plans, production estimates and schedule sheets, color swatches and paint chips. After a while money changed hands, and contracts were duly signed, and schedules were agreed upon, and we headed home to wait a few more days for the place I had waited for my whole life. On the way home, we took to calling the thing a studio.

I was glad to have the few days. I needed the time to make room in our garden for a room of my own. Which unfortunately meant that a few panels of the fence-that-never-knows-completion needed to come down.

———

I ended up taking down five sections of the fence along the alley. Two of them had to come down permanently to make room for the studio itself. The third one held the gate, which had to be moved since the studio was going in where the gate connected. The other two did not really have to come out, but they fell when I took the first three out. It occurred to me I could very well be putting this fence up for the rest of my life. I also wondered if two or three sturdy roses might help hold the whole business up.

Early one morning I was up to make sure the back garden was ready to receive the load of lumber for the studio, and the two folks who were to build it showed up. They turned out to be a man and his wife who live way out in Dickson County. They supplement their farm income by building prefabbed farm buildings in urban neighborhoods for city slickers like me to use as studios.

The first day they unloaded the materials, set the posts, and put down the plywood deck. The second day they framed it all in, including the roof. The third day they put on the tin roof and the exterior sheets of paneling, framed in the doorway, and hung the doors. By sunset on the third day, the three of us were sitting under the maple tree with a cold drink in our hands. They were admiring their handiwork. I was wondering if they could have built my fence in something less than eighteen months.

But it was a sight to behold.

———

The folks from Dickson said they had never actually built a tack room with french doors, but they otherwise seemed quite pleased with the whole business. They took pictures to put in their scrapbook. Then shaking their heads and grinning to themselves, they drove off.

To this day I am convinced I could have done the thing myself for no more than four times the cost and well within my standard three-year time frame for any construction project requiring more than a dozen two-by-fours. I hung my fence panels back up, hung my gate to the side of my three-day miracle, and held my tongue.

Early the next morning I took two cushions large enough to sit on, a sketchbook, a fountain pen, and a cup of coffee and went off to my little room to put a few words on paper and see if they would turn into something that would justify the name *studio*.

I finally had a little place of my own to hold the tools of my trade and dig around in.

Without meaning to, I helped to set off a building boom in Sunnyside.

John decided he needed a little building to keep his Harley in. Joan decided it was time for her to put the potter's studio in. Every time I go by Hal's house, there is a new pile of lumber being unloaded, and a crowd of workmen is building something in his backyard.

It could be they have just joined the lawn-elimination revolution. Or it could be they are building things they have always dreamed of.

Once the studio was finished, there followed a stretch of days and weeks and months in which I got up before daylight, spread out my writing things, and scribbled my pages for the day. Then I put my writer tools away and got out my carpenter tools and spent as many hours as I could hanging bead board on the interior walls of the studio. At the end of the day, I swept out the sawdust and put the tools back in the corner and stacked the lumber as neatly as I could so the place would be as serene as it could be for the writer's work the next morning.

Finishing the construction in the studio took some time. My crew had their hands full with softball and wrestling and high school by then, so I worked along as best I could on both projects, pounding away on a book in the mornings and hammering away on the walls and ceiling in the afternoons. The two kinds of work I did in that room that year, with the two different sets of tools and with the same two hands, yielded a book I eventually came to love and a fine place in which to try to make some more of them.

———

The bell at the front gate rang early one Saturday morning in spring, and I went to see who it was. Hal stood there with three cardboard boxes under one arm and a bag of stuff from Dwight's hardware store slung over the other. His fancy rolling tool chest was beside him.

"Happy birthday, boss," he said. No one has ever called me "boss" except Hal. "I've come to wire your studio."

Your neighborhood should have a Hal. He is not perfect by any stretch, except in the sense he is always perfectly Hal, which is more than enough for me. You cannot have ours, by the way; you must find your own. If there is not one in your neighborhood, you may want to consider becoming the one for your neighborhood. People will love you for it, and they will always grin when they see you coming.

Months passed before we actually hooked up the power to the studio, but we were ready when the time came because Hal made sure we were.

———

One day the studio was done. Not everything, of course, but the paneling was up, and the floor was finished out enough to move bookshelves in and rescue some of my books from storage. I was so tickled to see some of those old friends that I talked to them as I put them on the shelves. If gardeners can talk to roses, writers can talk to books.

One day I went to Dwight's and bought a huge canvas drop cloth and spread it out and stapled it to the floor. Another day I went and bought a big rug and spread it from wall to wall. Then I built a table to write on. And then the first of a long line of chairs started coming through.

Then the Rector arrived.

The Rambling Rector is a fine Old English rose, a climber that comes with an admonition to plant it next to a house or a tree. It will grow to about forty feet tall and twenty to thirty feet wide. It blooms once a year, early in the spring.

Someday it will cover my studio. For now, I still have to go out to the alley to see it, but in one or two more springs, I will come out the back door some April morning, and its white blossoms will have covered the studio roof.

I am willing to wait.

———

My room at the back of the garden serves as one part retreat, one part sanctuary, one part office, one part library, and one part storage facility. It is also the place I go to dig around with a pen each day, plant a word or a sentence, and see if something will grow and if it might become something beautiful.

A garden is not a bad place for such a place. Gardens are about waiting and about hope as much as they are about anything.

You wait for spring to come and for roses to bud out and for the earth to green up again. You wait for seeds to germinate and irises to spread. You wait for the dogwoods to turn white and pink and for the maple to go golden in the fall. And all the while you hold a vision of some new thing in your head, of what the garden will be someday.

You cannot hurry it along, not any of it. Spring comes when it comes; roses bloom when they will; the garden grows at its own sweet pace. What it teaches you is to wait, to be patient, and to pay attention.

Some morning the sun will rise, and something you have always dreamed of will come true.

SIX

Water Music

What gardener isn't of two minds?
Even as you are sighing with satisfaction
with what you have at last pulled off...
the other ambitious mind
is already making greedy notes
for what must be done next year.

—MIRABEL OSLER

Among the things pinned to my studio wall is a rough sketch, ink and colored pencil on tissue paper. I keep a postcard pinned there as well, a postcard we once sent to ourselves from St. Vincent in the Caribbean.

The sketch reminds me of a birthday present, and it eventually led me to a man who calls himself Mr. Shrub. The postcard reminds me of a particularly lovely vacation, and it led me to a man named Sammy. Between the sketch and the postcard and Mr. Shrub and Sammy, I stumbled onto a rarely stated piece of gardening wisdom I was previously unaware of: you can lead a gardener to water, but you cannot make him think.

———

Late on a fine afternoon in April, I was whistling to myself as I showered and changed after some light yard work.

I was whistling because I was being taken out to dinner for my birthday. It was not a surprise to be taken out to dinner that evening. At my age, my birthday is one of the few things I remember, and so it never sneaks up on me. I can hear its footsteps coming months away.

The whistling was appropriate too, because I thought I could begin to see the end of the major gardening projects. The fence was done, and the studio was finished. The flower beds were in place, and the roses were off and climbing their little hearts out. As far as I could tell that afternoon, the summer-yard work load was going to be relatively moderate. I had begun to envision a boccie ball court, but I was holding my tongue until the winter meetings with the master planner.

I put on some fresh linen clothes, pronounced myself ready to be celebrated, and we headed to our local, a fine little restaurant in the neighborhood that is always my favorite place to celebrate anything. Once we settled in, a scroll of tissue paper wrapped in a ribbon was handed to me. The attached card said some lovely things I will not tell you, because they are between me and the person who loves me. I *will* tell you about the tissue paper.

I unrolled the paper to discover the master planner had been sketching again. This time instead of sketching a new bed in the garden, she had drawn a sketch of a fountain. "It could not be delivered today the way I wanted it to be," she said. "The paint did not dry."

I was happy for the gift and comforted to know the fountain had already been made. My limited do-it-yourself skill set does not include welding.

"It will be delivered tomorrow," she told me. Somewhere during dessert it occurred to me that a seven-foot fountain likely needed a pond and someone needed to dig it. I began to rewrite the lyric to the traditional birthday song in my head: "…happy birthday, dear Robert, happy birthday to you…and here's your shovel."

———

The next afternoon a truck pulled up in the alley, and I went to the back gate, and in came the fountain. A fountain big enough and pretty enough to be in a park or in a courtyard of a house in the French Quarter. Four bowls with scalloped edges, swans around its base, freshly painted black and shining in the sun—it was beautiful. Then they brought in a black plastic tub to put into a hole to make a pond. They left without making the hole for the pond. Not a surprise really, though I had harbored a secret hope for eighteen hours or so.

By sunset we had picked the spot for the fountain. I had to travel for the next few weeks, so it was going to be awhile before I could dig the hole for the tub. But we could not wait to hear the water's music, so we just set the tub on the ground. Then I dragged and rolled and muttered the fountain across the yard at the blistering pace of about three feet per ten minutes. As I wrestled it over into the tub, I began to suspect it had once been in the same park in Cairo where the fence pieces in the rose garden had come from. I leveled it up as best I could and started filling the tub with water.

It was not yet as elegant looking as it was going to be once I had time to dig the hole and put some bricks around it, but the tinkling sound we heard when the water plopped from bowl to bowl and down to the pond fell on our ears as elegantly as any music we had heard in the backyard in a while. If we closed our eyes, we were in the French Quarter.

After some weeks passed, I emptied the tub and rolled the fountain out of the way. My children came home from camp, and the excavation began. ("Yes, your father's birthday is still being celebrated," I told them. "Now, grab a shovel and help him with his present.") Together we fought our way through the rock just below the surface and carved out the hole. Then we dropped the tub in.

Once the tub was filled and the fountain reinstalled, we pulled up lawn chairs and spent many an hour sitting and listening to it. We sat near it as though it were a hearth and stared at it the way you stare at a fire on a winter's evening. We loved listening to the water fall and watching the birds fly in and out of the sprinkles. We were mesmerized by it.

One morning as we were sitting in the shade by the fountain and plowing our way through the last pages of the *Times,* we came to the conclusion that if you have a fountain that looks like it belongs in a courtyard in the French Quarter, it is only right to build a courtyard to put it in. By the time we finished talking and dreaming and sketching, we needed a retaining wall with steps in the middle that led to a brick patio surrounding the fountain. We also needed to move far more dirt than I was willing to move armed with nothing but a shovel.

Enter Mr. Shrub.

———

His real name is Ray, and he owns a nursery about five blocks from our house. We had bought things there from time to time and had seen the brochures that promoted his landscaping business. In the neighborhood, we call him Ray. In the landscaping world, he is known as Mr. Shrub.

I asked if he could send someone down to my house with a Bobcat to move some dirt around for me. To be honest, I felt like I was having to talk him into it. I was willing to pay the fee, but he seemed to be hoping I might turn him loose to be Mr. Shrub in my yard. I was not about to allow anyone else to lay claim to the title of Mr. Shrub in my yard after all of the digging I had done.

We set a date that gave me a few days to get my son and one of his buddies to empty the water out of the tub and get the tub out of the ground. Early on the morning for the Bobcat work, I once more rolled and dragged the fountain out of the way. I sang a couple of choruses of "Happy Birthday" to myself as I once again wrestled the thing across the yard.

Of course, I had to pull part of the back fence down again in order to get the Bobcat into the yard. It was easier this time. Since taking my fence down every few months to get something large into the backyard seemed to be a regular part of gardening at my house, I bought a two-foot length of PVC pipe wide enough to hold a fence post, and I sank the pipe into the ground. Now it only takes about five minutes to remove sixteen feet of fence—unscrew the panels, drag them out of the way, and that middle post just pops right out of the ground. It is much easier on my back and on my emotional well-being.

The Bobcat came in through the hole in the fence with one of Mr. Shrub's landscaping crew at the wheel. Mr. Shrub followed him into the yard. We walked around for a few minutes, and I told him what I hoped to have done. Then he said about twelve words to the Bobcat guy and got in his pickup and left.

I spent the next few hours trying to make myself heard over the roar of a Bobcat ripping around my yard. He shoved the dirt around for a few minutes, and then I made some hand signals, and he shoved some more dirt. Then he backed into a hydrangea or something, and I frantically waved him to a stop, and he made the international yard worker signs for "I am so sorry" and went at it again. Finally, mercifully, the bank I hoped for began to take shape. And the Bobcat man drove off down the alley and up the street without looking back.

I wrestled my fence back into place and sat down to savor one of the great lawn elimination moments of my life.

Then the rains came. It rained for almost three weeks straight. Day after day, a hard, driving rain fell. There was so much rain that Mr. Shrub dropped by one day unannounced to loan me two hundred square feet of plastic to roll out over the mud so it had a chance to begin to dry out.

Three more weeks went by before the whole business dried out enough to dig another hole to put the fountain in—yes, Mr. Bobcat filled in the hole we had already dug.

We put the pine straw back in its place and did what do-it-yourselfers do when the going gets tough—we went on vacation.

—

The two of us have always taken a trip in October to celebrate our wedding anniversary. This particular year we were celebrating our tenth anniversary, so we made the choice to go somewhere exotic, St. Vincent in the West Indies.

We stayed in a small cottage with a private swimming pool about six steps from the back door of the cottage. It was a small pool, only four or five feet deep and about two good crawl strokes across. The brochure called it a plunge pool, but you could hurt yourself if you actually plunged into it. *Tiptoe-in pool* might have been a better term. But there was something ridiculously fine about being able to walk out your back door and cool off whenever you wanted to. We discovered something equally fine about standing in the pool and reading a book or sitting up to our waists in the water on the steps leading down into the pool and watching the sunset or the stars.

Inevitably, it seems now, we came to the conclusion that it would be a fine thing to have one of these in the back garden.

Hello, Sammy.

———

When spring came, we drew up revised sketches of the back garden and talked to some pool guys to see if what we wanted to be done could in fact be done.

One guy told us he thought so, but the next day he called and said he had changed his mind and he did not think it could be done after all. Another guy came to see us and graciously drank our iced tea at the table under the maple tree for two hours and told us that what we wanted to do could not be done. He could, however, see a way to do what he wanted to do in our backyard, and all it would take would be a year and a half and roughly the amount of money necessary to buy a beachfront condo in Miami.

Then Sammy showed up. He did not show up on the appointed day or the one after that either—a sign of things to come—but he did show up.

Sammy sat down at our table under the maple tree, and we started in on the iced tea, and two hours later we were walking off spaces in the yard and scribbling on the sketches and looking through pool catalogs. We chose a fiberglass pool. You just dig a hole and drop it into the ground, and in three days you are in the water. Or at least that is what Sammy told us.

By the end of the afternoon, papers had been signed, and our plunge pool was on the way. According to Sammy, in six weeks the pool would be here and three days later we would be plunging in it.

Six weeks later we were calling Sammy daily for updates on the arrival of our pool. The same was true when we hit the eight-week mark.

In Sammy's defense, the pool was actually manufactured in Florida and shipped up here on a flatbed truck. A couple of times word was that the factory had changed the delivery date. Then word came that it took longer because we had ordered a special color. Then we heard they were waiting on another pool to be finished so they could ship the two together. Finally we were told it had been shipped but the truck broke down in Atlanta. One afternoon they called to say that the pool would be here in the morning. The next morning they called to say the truck was stranded in a bad storm on Monteagle Mountain in East Tennessee where a rock slide had closed the road. More than a little discouraged by the unanswered telephone calls the next morning, we gave it up and went for a long, late lunch.

At four o'clock we came around the corner, and there they were—a van full of workers and tools, a pickup truck with a trailer carrying a backhoe, and a semitruck with a flatbed trailer loaded down with what seemed to be the largest bathtub I had ever laid eyes on.

Sammy jumped down out of the cab of his truck and flashed his "Here I come to save the day" grin. "I told you it was coming," he said. "Better get that fence down."

Sammy's army hit the ground too. In short order they backed the truck into the alley, and with several mighty heaves and a great host of, shall we say, colorful words of encouragement from their fearless leader, they shoved the twelve-by-sixteen-by-five-foot bathtub off the trailer and across the backyard and almost to the edge of the house. Looking at it standing there under the maple tree, I thought it might possibly take up the entire backyard.

In the meantime, Sammy began to do what we later agreed is the thing that, if it is not what Sammy does best, is the thing Sammy loves most—operate a backhoe. For the next two hours, shouting instructions over the roar of the engine to his guys in the hole, who were using shovels to show him the edges of the rocks, talking on the radio to his crews at other construction sites, and handling calls from his office on his cell phone, all at the same time, Sammy dug a hole for the pool. I do not know Sammy at all really, and so I know nothing of the way he grew up. But I am convinced he spent most of his childhood in the dirt playing with Tonka trucks and making engine noises and shouting instructions to his playmates. When he grew up, he simply got bigger toys to play with.

We watched as Sammy went back and forth with the backhoe. One guy dug small rocks out of the hole, two guys hauled PVC pipe and plumbing equipment into the yard while Sammy shouted instructions at them, and a man named Wendell was assigned to stand beside us, smoking one cigarette after another, interpreting what Sammy was saying and doing, and telling us not to worry.

At three and a half feet down, Sammy struck serious rock. It was not a surprise, but it was unsettling since the hole needed to be five feet deep. A portion of the continental shelf had evidently moved into our yard when our heads were turned. Sammy prodded the edge of it with the backhoe, and a corner of my studio moved in response. Sammy took the backhoe out of gear. A meeting was in order.

Sammy and Wendell and the master planner and I gathered around the hole to shout at each other over the roar of the backhoe's idling engine. The rest of the crew stopped what they were doing and stood off to the side to watch with some interest.

The discussion went on for a few minutes. I remember the word *dynamite* being used at least twice and shaking my head furiously as I contemplated Sammy the Tonka man being turned loose in our yard with explosives. After a few more minutes, during which I nearly reached the wailing and gnashing of teeth stage, the decision was made. The only logical choice was to set the pool on the rock and raise the dirt up around it. The dream of the French Quarter courtyard around the fountain and the gently curving wall disappeared forever. A disappointment to be sure, but one that paled in comparison to the thought of blowing up the backyard. Sammy's crew seemed a little let down by the news that they would not be breaking out the dynamite to break up the rock, I think, but they went back to work.

About six fifteen, Sammy backed the backhoe out into the alley and ran it up on the flatbed truck, and the driver roared off toward the interstate highway to get home to Dickson. I figured we were done for the day. But Sammy and the boys grabbed hold of the pool and sweated it into the hole. Then one of them started cutting holes for the pipes, and another man started connecting pipes to the pump, and everybody else started throwing dirt around the edges. At some point, Sammy shouted to Wendell to turn the hose on.

"It's going to take twelve hours to fill 'er up. We may as well get 'er started," he announced. "You'll be swimming in it day after tomorrow."

On the third day, the water reached the proper level, and the pumping system began to circulate the water, and we went for a swim after Wendell and the boys left for the day, just as Sammy said we would.

For another month, a portion of Sammy's crew showed up in our yard almost every day. They spread three dump trucks of gravel to set the pool; they poured concrete for the deck; they put brick coping around the edge of the pool. Every morning I wondered if our garden would ever be a quiet, peaceful place again. Then one day, nobody came. The Sammy show had closed.

My work had just begun. Again.

———

Before long, a new stretch of fence took shape to hide the pump from view, and we planted ornamental grasses to separate the pool from the rest of the yard. I built two sets of steps with old stone left over from Wally's yard.

The fountain was moved to a new spot; a new sketch appeared calling for a permanent pond I have not finished yet. Pine straw was spread to cover the mud until the next spring when we could plant the new beds we had begun to sketch onto the big chart.

But we could sit in the sun and then cool off in the pool. We could stand in the pool and read a book, and we could sit on the benches in the pool and have a conversation while the sun went down or the moon came up. We could eat dinner on the deck and float candles in the water. We could invite our friends for an afternoon swim, and we could lie on a float in the sun and listen to the sound of the solar fountain in the pool.

———

I learned some stuff that summer. I learned that Bobcats and backhoes are very loud machines. And I learned, for the third or fourth or fifteenth time, that putting up a fence is not a one-time event. At my house, it is more like an ongoing struggle.

I was reminded too, as if I had never noticed before, that just about the time you think you have all your ducks in a row, someone will show up with another one. You may even do this to yourself. It is hard enough to keep your ducks in a row when someone is scattering them; it gets really hard when your ducks seem to be multiplying. Somewhere there are places where things stay the same, but a garden is not one of them. At least not the one in our backyard.

As a general rule, for gardening and most other things as well, I recommend you keep your tools handy—something new is always coming, and there is always some more digging in to be done. Always put your tools away when you are done for the day, but do not put them too far away.

That summer I learned anew that there is something soothing about water in a garden. The sound helps to buffer the noise of the city, or provides a counterpoint to it is perhaps a better way of saying it. Being able to slip into the cool water at the end of a summer's day or take a dip before bedtime is a lovely thing. It is nothing less than a gift, pure and simple.

Others have gifts in their lives that mean as much to them as this gift does to me. One of our friends keeps a boat on a lake an hour or so from town, and he invites us up for the weekend sometimes. I told him that this is a lot of work to go to for a swim; one can do that closer to home. I have even offered him our sketches and Sammy's telephone number. But he is not trading. And I do not blame him.

As I am writing this, the rain gently falls on the tin roof of my studio and plops into the pool a few steps away, adding a steady bass note to the tinkling of the fountains.

And I am keeping one eye on the garden as I listen. Some new thing is coming.

SEVEN

Garden Parties

Invent your world.

Surround yourself with people, color,

sounds, and work that nourish you.

—SARK

W^{E ARE QUIET PEOPLE}. We generally choose for the stereo to be down low rather than up loud. We walk down the hall to announce dinner is ready rather than shout. We sit for hours reading books and hardly say a word to each other and call it a fine day. We have even been known to read books at the dinner table as we sit across from each other.

Some of our preference for quiet comes by way of personality. Some of it because we both work at home and need quiet; you never know when someone is on the telephone when you come through the door or is working on a paragraph in his head.

Some of it grows out of our shyness, though after all these years together now, we tend to be less shy around each other than we were. Some of it may reflect the fact that we both grew up with three brothers and a sister and quiet was hard to come by. We may still be in search of a little makeup peace and quiet after the years in a noisy household.

In addition to being quiet, our preference is to stay in rather than go out. It does not bother us to go for days without speaking to or seeing anyone other than each other, save talking to the children and staying in touch with clients and publishing people.

Oddly enough, we love to entertain. And once the weather starts to get warm in March and right on through to the middle of October or so, our favorite place to have company is in the back garden.

We started entertaining in our back garden almost as soon as we had a fence. In fact, the fence finally got painted because a major party had been announced, and invitations had been issued, and I had long since passed the time when my standard "The wood needs to season before I paint it" excuse passed for a reasonable one.

It took awhile to paint the fence.

———

For one thing, a fair amount of the fence is tucked up against the hedges on two sides of the yard. So the painting called for a brush rather than a spray-painting machine. The power painter, as the folks at the hardware store called it, proved useful for the privacy-fence panels and the studio, but when it came to painting spindles, the job called for two-inch brushes all the way. The power painter put more paint on your hedge and your roses than on your fence.

Between cutting pyramids and painting spindles, I believe my fence is one of the prettiest and most exasperating things I have done. It is a design triumph and a maintenance disaster.

I think I could have hiked to the Great Wall of China

and back in the same number of hours I spent that summer standing in the hot sun, sweat running down my face, holding the hedge or a rosebush back with one hand and dabbing on paint with a two-inch brush in the other hand. It seemed as though the fence was growing; every morning it looked longer and taller than it had the day before.

At least I still had my crew.

My daughter helped with the spindles, hard worker and kind soul that she is. And my son, lover of all power tools great and small, manned the spray painter. I prefer tools that do not have motors—I am a paint-with-a-brush, write-with-a-fountain-pen, cut-boards-with-a-handsaw sort of person. He likes machines, any machine, and the louder the better. I believe he fell in love with the power painter based on sheer volume. He took one look at the two-inch brush in my hand and the one-armed hedge-holding posture required to do the brushwork and announced he would happily power-paint the studio and the privacy fence. "Don't worry about it at all, Dad. I'll take care of the big stuff for you."

Summer days rolled past us with my daughter and me in the hedges and my son wailing away with the power painter. James Taylor joined us on the boom box. We invited him along because all three of us love him.

There was sunshine and sweat and Gatorade, and there was "Fire and Rain" on the stereo. And I was a happy yard guy and an even happier father. When the painting was done, the party was held, and I was a pretty proud host as well.

———

The next major festivity in our backyard just sort of snuck up on us.

We invited two of our friends to go with us to the local minor-league ballpark for an afternoon game. Then the four of us were coming back to our yard to grill out. Hardly a party. Even shy people know it takes more than four persons to qualify as a party.

We picked up two other neighborhood couples at the ballpark. While waiting on the grill to warm up, one of us was strolling the rose garden, and a neighbor stopped to say hello, and in a few minutes she headed back to the house for some more food and a spouse. Then the bell rang at the gate a few minutes later, and more friends came in. Another couple we know drove by and saw all the fun through the gate, so they came too. In a short while there were sixteen of us, a number that does indeed qualify as a party. A foraging detail was dispatched to purchase additional supplies.

Fortunately I had my great-grandfather's sample table.

In my family I am regarded as the guy you call when the stuff that belonged to one of our ancestors is about to be sold or thrown away. Every family has such a person.

There is an unwritten rule that after everyone else goes through the stuff and latches on to the useful stuff and the pretty stuff, then call Robert. I will take most all of the other stuff because I am the most sentimental of us all. It does not matter how old or how odd, if it came from the house of an ancestor, I will take it.

I do not know exactly why I am that way. I do know I prefer old rather than new. I like nicked and scratched and weathered more than I like new and shiny. The majority of my favorite things came to me with some character in them and on them. Not surprising considering the characters that appear on one or two of the branches of the family tree from which I have not fallen very far.

When I am working on the road, I carry with me a rosary given to my father before he died by a nun from a place he used to go on retreat. I do not say the rosary, and neither did he, but I was told he held it the night he died even though the nurse said that he may well have never known it. I have two sets of bookshelves in our front hall made out of cheap one-by-twelve pine. Pop built one set, and Wally built the other. They are painted in colors I do not like and are scratched and beat-up, but I will not paint over them. I use Wally's old pipe rack to hold my fountain pens in my studio. We use my grandmother's china in the dining room. And this is just the stuff that came from my family.

Sometimes it feels like I am living in a museum or at a yard sale.

———

When Wally died, his house had to be sold, and everyone else in the family went through the house and took away the treasures they wanted and the things that could be put to good use in their houses. Then I went through the house to see if I could find anything I wanted to take home.

The advantage to going last, of course, is that no one fights you for whatever you find.

Down in Wally's basement, pushed back into a long-neglected corner, was a low table. Actually it was only a frame with legs. The top had long ago succumbed to the years of neglect that accrued to anything sitting in a corner of Wally's basement. The table is twelve feet long and two and a half feet high.

My mother was in the basement with me, and so I asked her about the table. "It came from your great-grandfather's millinery shop downtown," she said. "He used it as a sample table to show hats on. You want that old thing?"

Years later, on a summer night in Sunnyside, sixteen of us, suddenly more friends than I have ever had in my entire life, were eating and laughing and talking and telling stories by candlelight under the branches of the big maple tree in our back garden. And we were sitting at that old table.

To me, the difference between an antique and an heirloom has to do with ownership. An antique is something that has been around a long time. It belonged to someone, was maybe even treasured by someone, but not by anyone you know. An heirloom, no matter how old or curious, belonged to someone you knew and loved. And when you are paying attention, there in your garden, on an afternoon with the light just so, or on an evening when your friends are with you and the laughter and the talk flow freely and the candles glisten brightly, you recall those loved ones, and they are with you again.

———

When we first moved to Sunnyside, we saw a lot of real-estate signs in the yards throughout the neighborhood. It seemed there was a house for sale in every block. These days the signs have changed. Every block has one of those signs announcing a recently delivered baby. There are children everywhere.

Our children do not have children yet, and so grand-parenthood has not descended on our house yet. It is fine with me if it waits awhile. I am not ready to be anyone's grandparent at the moment.

On the other hand, the master planner here suffers

from a case of what my father used to call the "can't hardlys." She cannot hardly wait until we have grand-children to come and visit. So she has begun to practice. One day she declared Baby Day at the pool.

She got in touch with all of the young parents of young children in the neighborhood and invited them to bring their children and come for a pool party. She went out and bought floats and water wings and stocked the outdoor kitchen with boxes of apple juice and crackers. The babies came and brought their parents with them, and she sat in the swing and laughed for hours. When we walk through the neighborhood now, little kids wave at her and ask when they can come to the pool. Her legend grows a bit each summer.

———

Sometimes the garden parties we hold are smaller and less rowdy. A long day of working in the yard will be finished off by just the two of us having dinner outside as the sun sets. Or my son, the budding young chef, will come by on his day off, and he will man the grill, and the three of us will take our dinner under the maple tree. I live with a good southern cook and have somehow raised a young man who is learning to be a chef, so if I keep my mouth shut and leave them alone, they feed me pretty well. It is not out of the ordinary for these impromptu supper parties to include my daughter when she is home from college. My mother lives only a few minutes away, and she has been known to come for supper in the garden too when she hears the two cooks are working that night.

Sometimes we will spread the word for a couple of blocks that the pool is open for the afternoon, and neighbors and friends will come by for a swim, and we will sit and laugh and tell stories all evening.

———

Ours is not the only household in Sunnyside that does such things. There are three serious Christmas parties within a few blocks of here each year, and some years there are at least four pancake breakfasts. One of our neighbors puts a sign in his front yard every couple of weeks or so—The Cozy Corner Café Is Open—a general signal to all of us to bring something for the grill and come on through his back gate.

There are at least two fish fries a year on our block, and whenever someone is moving away, we count on a farewell party being held at Todd's. Not to mention the annual crawfish boil offered up by two transplanted Louisianans who have dug in here pretty good themselves.

We also have a neighborhood association in Sunnyside, and each year there is a home tour. It is one part fundraiser for the association and one part self-promotion for the neighborhood itself. The real reason for the event is so we all have a chance to peek inside other people's houses to see what they did with their old houses that might be better than what we did with our old house. Then we have some indoor projects to work on at our house while we wait through the cold weather until we can get back in the yard.

One year we put our house and our garden on the tour. The reason you do that is so you will finish up all of the projects you have been putting off for months.

We spent several weeks frantically cleaning and painting and planting and fluffing. *Fluffing* being the decorator term for what you do when you are trying to make every corner of your house and yard look like something from a photo shoot in an interior-design magazine featuring rooms that seem to have never been lived in. Of course, it rained off and on the day of the home tour, and the thought of three hundred people with wet feet walking through the house seemed like a rather ignominious end to all the cleaning and fluffing, but nothing could be done.

The traffic plan we drew up called for people to come in the front door, go through the house in a circle, saying brilliantly complimentary things all the while, come out the back door into the garden and wander their way through it, and exit through the rose garden gate to the street. I spent the day in the garden in the rain while someone else stayed in the cozy house and listened to the compliments. But it was okay with me, because I got to answer questions about the garden and listen to people say things like "We had no idea this was back here."

"Can I move in here?" was a recurring question. (The answer to which was no, by the way, but I did tell them that if they had a cute baby who likes to swim, they might get to visit sometimes.)

My son came by for the day, as soon as he heard the cleaning and painting and fluffing were all done. He sat at the table under the maple tree for much of the afternoon, taking questions and explaining what he had been thinking when he designed this or that or the other in the garden. He charmed many a guest with the story of painting the fence or the moment when he knew that having the studio in that corner was the right choice. "I can't tell you how many times I redesigned this garden," I heard him say.

It seems all of those hours with the noise and the shaking of the power painter affected his memory in a way. But I was happy to watch him bask in the glow of the hard work he had done.

I was most certainly basking in the glow of it myself, if one can bask in a rain shower.

People wandered the path under the maple tree and past the brick patio we laid there. They came up the Wally stone steps to the pool deck and sat in the swing that overlooks the pool. Then they wandered over to the studio porch and peered in the screen doors to see what a room for a writer actually looks like. I have seen the same expressions on the faces of people at the monkey house at the zoo before. I told them the writer would be back for feeding time if they wanted to wait.

Some folks, when the rain let up for a moment, plopped down on a chair by the pool, in the sunroom so to speak, even though the sun did not make an appearance that day. Then they headed down the back steps and through the hydrangeas, which make the walls of the reading room, the shady spot where the crepe myrtles hang over the Adirondack chairs and the *Times* is consumed on warm summer mornings.

Then down the few steps past the fountain and into the rose room and out the gate. Whoever is in charge of the weather did not cooperate for the day's festivities, but the roses did; most of them bloomed early for the occasion. I do not know how the master planner pulled it off, but I was glad she figured out the right sweet somethings to whisper to them in the days before.

———

It was a day for remembering for me.

Someone would ask a question about how this thing or that came to be, and I remembered the sweat and the laughter and the cool drinks at the end of the day with my crew. I remembered Sammy and Mr. Shrub and the day the roses arrived, fragile and trembling and hopeful. I remembered my first morning in my studio and the day Wally's irises first bloomed. I remembered rolling the fountain across the yard and the day that my son and his buddy covered themselves in mud when they moved it so the Bobcat could get in.

I remembered the way not much at all grew or blossomed back here in the days when we first arrived, the children in tow, breathless and wide-eyed, hoping to make a home for us here. I remembered the days before the sketches, when these sweet garden rooms were still only dreams. I recalled the days when we knew no one here in Sunnyside, and now I can barely keep up with the names of all the friends who have found us here.

And I knew then that I was dug in here pretty well, had maybe even started to bloom in some sense. Enough so that like all gardeners, I have a case of the can't hardlys about how good all of this will look next spring and am already looking forward to it.

Uprooting me from here is going to take some work.

EIGHT

Morning Glories

For every man

the world is as fresh as it was the first day,

and as full of untold novelties for him

who has eyes to see them.

—THOMAS HENRY HUXLEY

M Y FAVORITE TIME TO BE IN OUR GARDEN is the
time before you can even see it. The time between four and five in the morning.

You cannot see the garden yet; it is still hidden in shadows. It rests in the dark, waiting for the sun and for the day
to start.

I like to be there then—sitting, listening for the symphony that will come, watching for the light that has been
promised, waiting for the show to begin. I am astonished
and grateful each time to have been plopped down into
this little corner of the Eden given again to us all each day.

Most mornings I do not need the clock to wake me up. I
find myself awake well before the alarm, lying in bed in the

dark, waiting until a reasonable hour to rise. *Reasonable* is a relative term, or so I am told by those who cannot believe that I rise that early.

I remember Pop saying he used to lie in bed in the dark, waiting for the sun to come up so he could get out of bed. Being a high-school student at the time, I thought he was crazy. Now I realize he was only middle-aged, an age I seem to have reached myself sometime ago. *Middle-aged* strikes me as a relative term; I do not think it likely I will live to be 108.

There are some good things about being my age and some not-so-good ones. Going out the screen door and down the steps into the garden, I remember that being up in the dark and waiting on the light clearly ranks as one of the good things.

According to the Ancient Story, "Let there be light" is all it took to begin to create the first of all places to which anyone ever belonged, the first of all the Edens. *This is as close as I am going to get,* I think as I start along the path toward the studio.

I open the double doors, set my coffee cup down, and take a seat facing out into the garden. Then I wait for the symphony to begin and the light to come up and the set to be revealed and the characters to appear on stage.

———

The opening notes of each day's symphony are percussion.

The fountain splashes down into a pool lined with small rocks I hauled home from retreats over the years. Certain rocks call to mind certain places and times. Better yet, they call to mind those who shared those days and moments with me. I think of it as a photo album, except that all of the pictures of these people and these places to which I belonged for a time are kept only in my heart.

The fountain pings and plops, ringing like a bell. On

mornings with a breeze, the ringing mingles with the sound of the wind chimes.

The next sounds in the symphony come from inside the hedges. The hedges hold the nests of the birds who call our yard home. Chirps and cheeps and whistles and calls fill the air, a whole reed section tuning up for the day's work.

A mockingbird lives in the maple tree. His specialty is to mimic the beep, beep, beep sound the security system makes when I come out the back door. More than once I have been sitting in my studio and heard it and looked up to see who was coming out into the back garden at this hour. This particular mockingbird particularly enjoys mocking me. He also imitates the squeak the screen door makes when I need to oil the hinges, a useful practice that almost makes up for his less-than-respectful general attitude toward me.

House finches are next, noisy folks who travel in packs and chatter a mile a minute with no regard as to whether the other finches are listening to them at all. A family reunion or an argument or a food fight roars to life every other minute with them. In between their frenetic bursts, you can hear the deep-throated calls of mourning doves as they make their stately strolls across the yard. The wrens who live under the studio roof are usually the last of the birds to join in the song. I do not know if wrens sleep late everywhere, but they do in our yard.

———

The light begins to come up, and so the colors of the set begin to come into view.

Tennessee is not big-sky country, not until you get out west toward Memphis, so the dawn goes on for quite a while at my house.

Depending on the time of year, and the angle of the sun in relation to the earth, and the number of leaves on the trees scattered through our neighborhood, a one- to two-hour gap falls between the time you can see the first streaks of light against the gray and the time you can actually see the sun itself. The sun does not just pop up here, the way it does at the shore or out west. It meanders its way through the hills that encircle our fair city.

What you can see, though, while you wait to see the sun itself, is pretty good.

The growing light slowly reveals the deep greens of the hostas in the shade beds beside the studio, and the browns and reds and terra cottas of the bricks and the pine straw.

The water in the pool in front of the studio begins to shine clear against the black of the pool itself and the gray of the tiles. Soft yellows and greens slowly appear in the great clumps of grass we planted to screen the front of the garden from the pool. The wrought-iron table and chairs show their deep green against the red-brick patio in the center of the garden, up under the maple tree. The shadow and light of the hedge catch my eye.

I can see the faint lines of the crepe myrtles. The first bits of bright color break through the shadows: the lavender beside the patio, the irises by the house, the hydrangeas along the fence. Finally the rose garden comes into view. Their reds and pinks and whites begin to wink at me from across the way.

Depending on the time of year and the temperature of the air, the garden glistens with dew or waits shrouded in mist. Sometimes the whole world, it seems, shines bright with frost. Sunnyside is not exactly the forest primeval, as Longfellow once referred to an Eden far more majestic than this, but at this moment the garden I gaze into is at least elemental—first light, first sounds, and mist and shadow and water and green.

———

I do not know what your portion of Eden looks like, nor do I know what it sounds like each day as it blinks and shuffles and murmurs and whistles its way into being. I will say this: it is the portion of the Eden that you have been given for this season of your journey.

The portion of Eden that I have been given is fairly modest—and it is more than I ever hoped for.

———

We spend most of the hours of most of our days here, at this little house, in this little garden. We work here and we weed here and we see our friends here. We watch the seasons come and go here. We celebrate our milestones and moments here. We rest here and we talk here and we plot out new bits of our life together in the rooms of this very garden.

These sweet rooms are the stage for almost all of my life. I am as dug in here as anywhere I have ever been. If this is not home, then no place will ever be. If this is not the last place for me, then at least I have learned something here, something of what it means to make a home anywhere at all.

It is a small house in a small garden in a small neighborhood. But it is large enough for us. Large enough to hold our dreams and our hopes and our joys and our sorrows. Large enough to hold our family and our friends and our neighbors from time to time. Large enough to hold our work and our rest and our tears and our prayer and our laughter and our silence and our wonder.

Large enough to hold nearly everything dear, or so it seems to me on mornings when I am up waiting on the light.

———

The beep, beep, beep sounds again, for real this time, and the lady to whom I am married comes out to stroll the rose garden to see who has bloomed since yesterday. I hear her say hello to the roses and the birds. And then she is up the steps and across to the studio doors to say good morning to me.

The final chorus of the morning hymn has been sung, and the light of the day is now fully upon us.

Who knows what this day may yet bring—who will

come to see us, what work will need to be done, what new thing is in store. All of it will be the life to which we have been given in this place, this place where we have dug ourselves in.

The life to be lived here this day, the life in which we live and move and have our being, as the old prayer book says, is right here in our own backyard. And it must be nurtured, it must be watched over, and it must be tended to.

AUTHOR'S NOTES

As solitary as it seems sometimes—both to me and, I suspect, to people who do not write—writing a book is not always a solitary pursuit. The best days are those when someone joins you in the work, a trait shared with the act of gardening as well.

Some days other writers and their books will come and join you. If you like digging around in your own backyard, building something to make a garden room, or other such things, I recommend the books listed below.

The Country Garden by John Brookes

Pilgrim at Tinker Creek by Annie Dillard

A Garden from a Hundred Packets of Seed by James Fenton

Dirt Under My Nails by Marilee Foster

Sweet Days and Roses by Leslie Geddes-Brown

Botanica's Roses, published by Laurel Glen Publishers

The Tool Book by William Bryant Logan

100 Old Roses for the American Garden by Clair Martin

A Place of My Own and Second Nature by Michael
 Pollan

The Rose Bible by Rayford Clayton Reddell

The Potting Shed by Linda Joan Smith

The Tiny Book of Tiny Houses by Lester Walker

My experience with this group of books is that at the very least they make you want to go put your yard clothes on and head out the back door. They will also teach you a lot of things about the life you will find and can tend to when you get there.

———

Sometimes other people will put their yard clothes on and help you with your work, provide goods and services that you cannot do without, give you gifts to put in your yard, or otherwise pitch in to make up for your shortcomings with a hammer and a trowel and a shovel.

The yardman that I am cannot write about our garden, think about our garden, or even walk through our garden without being grateful to Austin, Bill, Bo, Brenda, Brock, Dwight and company, Geoff, Glenn, Grant, Hal, Harold, JB, John & Wendy, Jordan, Justin, Kim, Michael, Peggy, Ray & the folks at Mr. Shrub, Sammy & his guys from Dickson, and William.

———

The writer that I am trying to be could not write a sentence, finish the work, or hold this one in his hands without the kind attentions of Ms. Jones of Merigold, Ms. Lil of Linda Lane, Ms. Dupree of Arab, and Ms. Carol of Euless. Even if it were possible, I would rather have done it with all of you at my side.

And you could not hold it in your hands without the

kind attention of Steve, Dudley, Jeanette, Sara, Ginia, Karen, Carol, Carie, and a whole host of kind and generous folks from WaterBrook Press and the rest of the world known as Random House.

Thank you, one and all, and the same to the Friends of Silence & of the Poor, whoever and wherever you may be.

NAMASTÉ,

R. Benson
Sunnyside, 2006

ABOUT THE AUTHOR

ROBERT BENSON lives and writes and tends to his garden in Nashville, Tennessee. He is always happy to get notes from fellow gardeners, fellow pilgrims, and other folks who are paying attention to the world around them. He even looks forward to writing back and will actually do so.

Please feel free to write to Robert at 1001 Halcyon Avenue, Nashville, TN 37204.

Or visit him, learn about his other books, inquire about speaking engagements, and otherwise see what he is up to at *www.robertbensonwriter.com.*

To learn more about WaterBrook Press and view
our catalog of products, log on to our Web site:
www.waterbrookpress.com

Midwives On-Call at Christmas

*Mothers, midwives and mistletoe—
lives changing for ever at Christmas!*

Welcome to Cambridge Royal Hospital—
and to the exceptional midwives
who make up its special Maternity Unit!

They deliver tiny bundles of joy on a daily
basis, but Christmas really is a time for
miracles—as midwives Bonnie, Hope,
Jessica and Isabel are about to find out.

Amidst the drama and emotion of babies
arriving at all hours of the day and night,
these midwives still find time for some
sizzling romance under the mistletoe!

This holiday season, don't miss the festive,
heartwarming spin-off to the dazzling
Midwives On-Call continuity
from Mills & Boon Medical Romance:

A Touch of Christmas Magic
by Scarlet Wilson

Her Christmas Baby Bump
by Robin Gianna

Playboy Doc's Mistletoe Kiss
by Tina Beckett

Her Doctor's Christmas Proposal
by Louisa George

Dear Reader,

This book is the first I've written as part of a continuity, and it was fun and challenging. I really enjoyed the way the editors came up with story ideas and connected the different books. It would have been hard to choose which hunky hero I wanted to write about, so I'm thrilled I was given sexy Aaron Cartwright to fall in love with in my story.

The other authors in the series set up an online chat so we could discuss the storylines and ask questions of each other. A thank-you shout-out to Louisa George, Scarlet Wilson and Tina Beckett for their help— particularly Scarlet, who, as the only author in our group currently living in the UK, was always happy to answer the numerous questions I had about medicine and midwives in England as compared to the US…and there were plenty of surprising differences.

Aaron and Hope share an attraction they've felt just from noticing one another in the hospital corridors even before they officially meet. When they finally do, it's *zing* with a capital 'Z'! But both have baggage from their pasts that make a relationship impossible. Not to mention Hope's secret plans to have a baby on her own through IVF very soon—a decision that rips open Aaron's old wounds when he finds out. But a fling isn't a relationship, right? Or so they think…! :)

I hope you enjoy Hope and Aaron's story—and the way they both come to see that the things they've always believed about themselves aren't necessarily true. Learning this isn't easy, and it takes falling in love with one another to see it.

I'd love to know what you think of this story! You can email me at Robin@RobinGianna.com, find me on my website, robingianna.com, or look me up on Facebook.

I look forward to hearing from you!

Robin xoxo

HER CHRISTMAS BABY BUMP

BY
ROBIN GIANNA

First published in Great Britain 2015
By Mills & Boon, an imprint of HarperCollins*Publishers*
1 London Bridge Street, London, SE1 9GF

Large Print edition 2016

© 2015 Harlequin Books S.A.

Special thanks and acknowledgement are given
to Robin Gianna for her contribution to the
Midwives On-Call at Christmas series

ISBN 978-0-263-26093-9

After completing a degree in journalism, working in the advertising industry, then becoming a stay-at-home mum, **Robin Gianna** had what she calls her 'midlife awakening'. She decided she wanted to write the romance novels she'd loved since her teens, and embarked on that quest by joining RWA, Central Ohio Fiction Writers, and working hard at learning the craft. She loves sharing the journey with her characters, helping them through obstacles and problems to find their own happily-ever-afters. When not writing, Robin likes to create in her kitchen, dig in the dirt, and enjoy life with her tolerant husband, three great kids, drooling bulldog and grouchy Siamese cat. To learn more about her work visit her website: robingianna.com.

Books by Robin Gianna

Mills & Boon Medical Romance

Changed by His Son's Smile
The Last Temptation of Dr Dalton
Flirting with Dr Off-Limits
It Happened in Paris…
Her Greek Doctor's Proposal

Visit the Author Profile page at millsandboon.co.uk for more titles.

This one is for you, Flora Torralba!

Thanks so much for your steady willingness to help in any way, for tolerating my nuttiness, and for keeping me sane.

I don't know what I'd do without you— you're the best! xoxo

**Praise for
Robin Gianna**

'If you're looking for a story sweet but exciting, characters loving but cautious, if you're a fan of Mills & Boon Medical Romances, or looking for a story to try and see if you like the medical genre, *Changed by His Son's Smile* is the story for you! I would never have guessed Robin is a debut author: the story flowed brilliantly, the dialogue was believable and I was thoroughly engaged in the medical dramas.'
—*Contemporary Romance Reviews*

CHAPTER ONE

"HELLO, KATE? IT'S just me." Hope Sanders gently knocked on the door and stepped inside her patient's room. "Let's check and see how it's going, shall we?"

Kate kept sucking on her ice cube and just stared, apparently so exhausted she couldn't conjure up any kind of response. Hope gave her a positive smile, sending up a silent prayer that, this time, the poor woman would finally be ready to deliver. After thirty-six hours of labor, any soon-to-be mother was beyond ready, mentally and emotionally, but sometimes her body and her baby just wouldn't cooperate the way everyone wished they would.

"Are you feeling all right?" Hope asked as she washed her hands and snapped on green examination gloves. "Contractions any worse or more frequent?"

"I'm not sure. I just want the baby out. Why can't you get it out?" Kate asked in a tearful voice.

"I know. It's been a long time, hasn't it?" Hope gave Kate's huge belly a gentle pat. "And you've been so tough throughout all these hours. But you're making good progress, so the doctor and I are pretty positive we can avoid a C-section. Maybe you're there now, so let's see."

"I'm sorry," Kate said, sniffing back her tears as Hope began an internal exam. "I shouldn't snap at you like that. Why on earth did you want to become a midwife and have to deal with cranky women like me?"

"First, you're not cranky, believe me. You've been very brave and stoic all this time." And the truth of that made Hope smile as she thought of the many mums who'd been so far past cranky during labor that there wasn't a word for it. "I enjoy helping mums through the difficulty of labor and delivery, and on to the joy of getting to hold their newborns for the first time. There's nothing as beautiful as a baby, is there? That's exactly why I became a midwife."

As she said the words the truth of that statement, and the emotion that came with it, closed her throat. Was she really, hopefully, about to have a baby of her very own? What she'd dreamed of when she'd first studied midwifery? When she'd thought she had all the time in the world to establish her career before having children, never imagining she'd still be alone at thirty-four?

"Well, you've been great, Hope, helping make all these hours more bearable," Kate's husband said. "We really appreciate it."

"Thank you. That means a lot to me." Hope's findings from the internal exam sent a huge sigh of relief from her lungs. She gave Kate a big smile she didn't have to force this time. "Guess what? Great news! You're there, Kate! Fully dilated at ten centimeters. Baby has decided she's ready to come into the world."

Kate kept licking her ice cube, almost as if she hadn't heard Hope, but her husband practically leaped out of his chair and came to stand by the bed. The poor man had dark circles all around his eyes and was about as disheveled as a person could look, but his beaming smile banished his obvious fatigue.

"You mean the baby's coming? It's time?"

"It's time. I'm putting a heart-rate monitor

around your belly, Kate, so we can see how baby is doing during delivery," Hope said as she strapped it on, praying this final stage went a lot more smoothly and quickly than the previous hours. "We need to get pushing. Can you give me a push next time you feel a contraction? I know you aren't feeling them as strongly because of your epidural, but tell me when you do."

"I...I'm having one," she said, sitting up straighter and looking alert now.

"Then give me a push. That's it. Well done. Again." Hope kept giving her gentle encouragement and checking her progress, pleased the fetal monitor showed the baby's heart rate was normal. Maybe after the long ordeal, this delivery really would be quick and easy. "Wonderful! Nice job."

Kate moaned and pushed as her husband clutched her hand. "Breathe now, love. Breathe."

"Yes, Kate," Hope said. "Take a breath between contractions. Puff, puff, puff. Then during a push, tuck your chin down, hold your breath and give it all you've got."

Kate worked hard, and Hope kept her tone soothing and encouraging, knowing if she exuded a relaxed composure it helped the mother in labor stay composed, too. After only a few more contractions, the top of baby's head was suddenly there, visible, and Hope sent mum another huge grin. "She's crowning! Almost here, Kate. Give me a push. You're doing a great job. Okay, I've got her head. One more push now. One more. Yes! You did it!" She wrapped her hands around the baby's shoulders and helped her slide out into her new world.

Hope's heart leaped into her throat as she held the slippery infant. No matter how many times she did this, the wonder of it, the miracle, hit her every single time, filling her chest with elation.

"Here she is, Mum! Perfect and beautiful. Congratulations." She laid the infant on Kate's chest, letting them marvel over their new little one for just a moment. "You were wonderful, even after being so tired. I'm so proud of you!"

Kate held her baby close, murmuring and cooing, and Hope hated to disturb the sweet moment. "I'm sorry, but I need to take her, as we don't want her to get chilled. We'll get her cleaned up and warm, then I promise I'll have her back to you in a jiffy."

As she lifted the baby from her mother's chest

and placed her on the cloth her assistant held, Hope saw tears sliding down the new father's cheeks as he leaned down to kiss his wife.

A pang of something sharp stabbed at Hope's heart. Regret, maybe, that she'd never experience that? That her own baby, if she was blessed with one soon, wouldn't have a daddy who wept at its birth and was there as he or she grew up? And all because of Hope's physical and emotional inadequacies?

She sucked in a calming breath and attended to Kate as the nurse assistant placed the baby in the bassinet beneath the heat lamp. She rubbed her all over until she was clean and rosy, slid a little knit cap onto her tiny head, then swaddled her in blankets. Hope lifted the infant into her arms, pausing for a moment before taking her to her daddy.

Serious blue-gray eyes stared up at her with a frown furrowing her tiny brows, as though she was asking Hope where in the world she was and why she was there. As Hope looked at the tiny, vulnerable new life she pictured her very own baby in her arms. The thought sent a thrill surging through her veins, warring with an icy fear that seemed to freeze her blood at the very same time.

She was close, so close, to that dream if she went through with her plans. But would her own child look to her with those same questions in its eyes? Who am I, and why am I here? Would she be able to answer, *You're here because I love you*? Would she be the kind of mother she wanted to be?

She tore her gaze from the precious one staring accusingly at her and took the baby to her parents, placing her gently into her father's arms.

"Your new daughter. Congratulations again."

Both stared at their newborn in awe as Hope swiped her cold hands down her scrubs. Terrifying doubt choked her. Would making a baby of her own be the right decision, or would it be a horrible mistake?

She fiercely shook off the sudden and disturbing doubts. She'd wanted a baby forever. Adored babies. Adored children, too. She was running out of time for that dream to come true, and despite her history, despite what her old boyfriend had said, there was no reason on earth to fear that she might not be capable of being the loving mother she so wanted to be.

Prayed she could be. Would be.

"She's so beautiful." Kate's husband looked at his wife. "She looks like you, I think."

Kate laughed. "Am I that pink and puffy right now? Probably, yes." She reached to stroke the baby's cheek, her voice becoming a whisper. "You were an awful lot of effort, but you were worth it, sweetest one."

She and her husband shared a long, intimate smile, and Hope felt that irritating pang jab her again. What was wrong with her? Why the sudden sadness over not having a man in her life, when she clearly had never wanted one? Why the ridiculous doubt when she'd been happy and confident before?

"Have you picked out a name for her?" Hope asked, busying herself with the final things that needed to be done for Kate post-delivery. Distracting herself with small talk was sure to banish these peculiar and unwelcome feelings swirling around her belly.

"Nine months didn't seem like long enough to

decide," Kate said with a grin. "But we finally whittled it down to either Emily or Rachel."

"I'm fond of the more traditional names, and those are both very pretty."

"Here, love, you hold her for a bit." Her husband placed the baby in Kate's arms and stared at the infant with his brows creased. "She's...she looks like a—"

"Rachel," they both said simultaneously, then laughed.

"Perfect," Hope said, her throat absurdly clogging up at this scene that could have come straight from a chick flick. Lord, you'd think she hadn't delivered hundreds of babies in her career. Or that she'd already received the upcoming hormone injections, with these kinds of silly emotions pinging all over the place.

Probably should buy some stock in a handkerchief company right now. If this kept up, for the next nine months she'd be sobbing all over her patients with every healthy delivery.

"You're all set now, Kate." She stripped off her gloves and managed to smile at the giddy new parents. "I'll be back in a bit to see how you're doing."

Hope headed down the hospital corridor to write up her notes on Kate and baby Rachel and glanced at her watch, glad to see her shift was almost over. And for once her Friday night would be filled with something more than just a casual dinner with friends.

Tonight was the big gala fund-raiser organized by one of the hunkiest doctors at Cambridge Royal Hospital. Not only was the man absurdly good-looking, Aaron Cartwright apparently cared about children, too, creating the foundation that promoted adoption in and around Cambridge. Plus, he'd been nice enough to invite several midwives and obstetricians from the hospital to share a few adoption stories their patients had experienced, knowing some financial donors might be interested in hearing them.

Hope had long admired Aaron Cartwright from afar, starting the very first day she'd spotted him in the hospital three years ago, stopping mid-step to do a double take at the man. He might be a man with a bit of a playboy reputation, but who cared? A woman didn't have to be in the market for a relationship to enjoy looking at a heartthrob.

Tonight she'd finally get to meet the dreamy

doc, who half the women in the hospital swooned over. While enjoying champagne and yummy food and dancing, before the start of her new life.

The bounce began to come back to her step as she walked into her office. What could possibly be a more perfect Friday-night distraction to get her mind back on the right track?

"You're going to be late if you don't finish up soon."

Aaron Cartwright looked up from the pamphlets he'd been grabbing from a drawer outside an exam room to see Sue Calloway frowning at him. Her lips were pursed and her hands held several clothes hangers filled with his tux, shirt, bow tie and cummerbund. "Isn't organizing my wardrobe outside an office manager's job description?"

"Nothing's outside my job description and you know it," she said. "You've been with your patients almost an hour already, and everyone's going to be wondering where you are."

"No one will be wondering about me. They'll all be happily eating and drinking and won't even notice when I show up." He gently tapped the top of her head with the brochures. "Don't worry, though, we're almost done. This couple is nervous, and need a little more TLC before they're ready to go home. I'm giving them loads of stuff to read to keep them occupied, even though I already gave them plenty."

"When is their IVF procedure scheduled?"

"This Tuesday. And now I'm going back in there, unless you want to give me more grief and make me even later."

"Well, hurry, then," she said in a testy voice, her twinkling eyes belying her tone. "I'd give you a little shove to get you going if I could, except my arms aren't free. Don't keep me standing here holding your finery forever."

He chuckled, shaking his head as he headed back into the room. Not too many other doctors were lucky enough to have someone like Sue to run the office—and his schedule—like a drill sergeant.

The anxious expressions on the couple sitting in the consulting room showed Aaron he hadn't alleviated their worries. But with the latest advances in fertility techniques and a little luck, the procedure he'd proposed could work for them.

He sat and put on his most reassuring smile,

handing them the additional brochures on in vitro fertilization and the newest technique he was recommending. "I understand this has been a stressful and difficult struggle for both of you, but now that we know exactly what's going on there's a better than good chance you'll be able to conceive."

"How many times have you done this ICSI procedure, Dr. Cartwright?" John Walters asked.

"More times than I can count. And the success rate of ICSI is a solid ninety percent. In fact, my success rate has been even higher than that, if I can toot my own horn a little." He smiled again. "As I told you before, I'm a big believer in this procedure. Under circumstances like yours, it's much better than the shotgun approach of traditional IVF."

John's lips were pressed into a grim line, and Aaron reached to squeeze his shoulder. Infertility issues were hard on everyone, but many men had a more difficult time dealing with it when it was due to their physical issues, as opposed to their wives'. As though it made someone less of a man, which of course it didn't. There were all too many men who made babies only to abandon them, and plenty of others who were donors but in no way could be considered fathers. Whose children would never know where they came from.

"I know you said you will only implant two eggs, but I still think we should implant more than that," Angela said, clutching her husband's hand. "I mean, it gives us a better chance of having one take, right? And if we ended up having multiple babies, we'd be more than happy about that."

"You think now that you would, but multiples are harder on the mother's body. More likely to lead to preterm birth with complications resulting from that, as well as serious birth defects. Not to mention that caring for triplets or quads can be harder than anyone imagines."

Harder than his own biological mother ever imagined. Even harder on her children, ending with tough consequences for all of them.

"I know, but still. I feel like this could be our last chance. So why not, when we're ready to accept whatever happens?"

The dormant emotion that occasionally surged to the surface and threatened his cool at times like this always took him by surprise. It had all happened so long ago, so why? Maybe he was like a sapling that had seeded next to barbed wire. He'd still managed to grow strong, absorbing it inside until it was invisible, but the sharp pain could still deeply stab when he least expected it.

He drew a long breath, battling to keep his voice calm. Firm and authoritative without verging on dictatorial. But he believed it was an important part of his job, a critical part, to help patients make responsible decisions, no matter how desperate they were for a baby.

"I appreciate that this has been a long and difficult process for both of you, Angela. And as I said before, if you want to work with another specialist who feels differently than I do on this subject, I will completely understand if you prefer to do that. You wouldn't have to start all over again—there are several doctors in this hospital I can refer you to, giving them your history and information on the meds you've been taking. I would guess someone else would be available to do the ICSI procedure soon."

"No," Angela said, shaking her head. "Everyone has told us you're the best at the ICSI procedure, Dr. Cartwright. I'm just…I'm worried that with only two eggs, none will take."

"And I'm not going to deny that that's possible, but we can try again, remember? One healthy, full-term baby, two at the most, is the goal."

"Yes. A healthy baby is all we want." She gave her husband a tremulous smile. "How long is nine months from next week? I better make sure everything's ready."

"Early August. A good birthday month, since it's yours, too." The return smile he gave her was strained. "Though everything's been ready for a long time, hasn't it?"

"A long time."

Her voice quavered, and tears filled her eyes. Aaron handed her a tissue he pulled from the box he always kept next to him. The pain and depression, grief and failure that couples struggling with fertility problems felt was often profound. He'd do the best he could to help these two people have the baby they longed for.

And pray they'd be mentally and emotionally prepared for that baby when it came.

He resolutely shoved down the old, faded memories that for some damn reason insisted on resurfacing today and refocused on his patients. He was pretty confident that the ICSI procedure would work for them. That he wouldn't need to nudge them to think about adoption, the way he did with couples unable to conceive even after medical science had tried everything.

Adoption. The word reminded him that Sue was waiting with his tux, and that, even though he was sure nobody would be worrying about his late arrival, he did want to speak earlier at the adoption fund-raiser he'd organized, rather than later. People loved seeing his slide presentation that showed foster kids becoming a permanent part of happy families, and were even more generous with their donations to plump the foundation's coffers.

Aaron resisted the urge to glance at his watch. As he'd told Sue, he'd never cut short a meeting with any patient for any reason. Every one of them deserved to be able to ask as many questions as they needed to feel comfortable prior to any procedure. Questions he always answered honestly, even it if was an opinion patients weren't always ready to hear.

"Thanks so much, Dr. Cartwright." John stood

and shook Aaron's hand, he and his wife now smiling real smiles. "We'll see you next week for the big day."

"Which will hopefully result in an even bigger day next August," Angela said.

"See you Tuesday morning at eight-thirty." Aaron opened his office door, and as soon as the patients began walking down the short hall to the office exit Sue appeared again.

"Better get spiffed up fast. You might think none of the highbrow folks at your fund-raiser will wonder why dynamic fertility expert and adoption advocate Dr. Aaron Cartwright is the last to arrive, but I know you want plenty of time to pass the hat. Expert though you are at squeezing cash from the most miserly turnip."

"Is that a criticism or a compliment?" He had to laugh, at the same time hoping it was true, since every donation helped. "I appreciate you sticking around and getting everything ready. So have you changed your mind about attending?"

"Too rich for my blood at three hundred quid a ticket. Six hundred if I bring Paul."

"You know you're both on my guest list. You

just like to play the poor, hard-working office manager who isn't paid enough to look after me."

She grinned at him. "And how do you know me so well after only three years?"

"Maybe because those exact words come out of your mouth almost daily." He grinned back. "Come on. Grab a dress and your husband and come have fun. You handled all the details for the thing practically single-handedly. Thanks to you, the band and the food will be great. Besides, you can keep me out of trouble."

"Another job that's too hard." Her eyes twinkled as she patted his arm. "Thanks for putting me on the guest list. And the OBs and midwives who have adoption stories to share, too—that's so smart of you. But Paul doesn't enjoy things like that, and I don't want to go without him. I'm sure it'll be a huge success just like last year, though. I hope you get lots of new donors and enjoy yourself."

"Fine. Don't be jealous when I'm in the newspaper photos of the gala and you're not."

"As if I'd be in them anyway. They just want pics of the handsome American doctor who helps patients conceive the baby they want, advocates for adoption of adorable children and who just might be dancing with a beautiful woman."

"They're destined for disappointment, then. There'll be too many people to talk into donating more for me to be distracted by a woman."

"Unless the right woman is there to distract you. Which I know does happen periodically, though you never let them hang around long, poor things. You're the most uncatchable doctor in this entire hospital." She winked. "Hurry and get dressed now. You're already past late."

"Yes, Mom." He took the clothes she shoved into his arms and had to smile at the way she mothered him. Not unlike the way his adoptive mother had, despite how messed up he'd been as a kid, which was challenging as hell for both his parents.

Thankfully, traffic wasn't quite as bad as usual, and he made it to the hotel quicker than he'd expected. He took a second to catch his breath, surveying the elegantly appointed ballroom.

It was decorated for Christmas with tasteful table decorations of silver and gold balls in sleigh-shaped containers. Shiny twigs and sparkly something-or-others were tucked between them, and red, pink and white poinsettias sat everywhere in eye-catching groups. Big-band music filled the room, the fifteen-piece orchestra he'd hired in full swing. Glittery Christmas trees stood here and there on the edges of the room, flanking the equally glittery women and tuxedo-clad men.

Aaron smiled. Sue had outdone herself. Might just be a record crowd of well-heeled guests, most of them smiling, talking and nibbling on hors d'oeuvres, clearly enjoying themselves.

Opening their wallets, too, which was the whole reason for this event. November was a little early for a Christmas party, but it was better not to compete with all the December holiday stuff going on out there. He had to admit he was proud that, in just three years, this event had become the must-go-to social extravaganza of Cambridge, with people coming from quite a few places well beyond the city. Paying for top-notch entertainment and food was necessary to attract the kind of attendees he needed to reach his fund-raising goals.

His stomach growled as he watched someone take a bite of chicken on a stick. Better grab some food before his belly embarrassed him as he tried to talk to guests. He took a little of everything so he could eliminate any mediocre items from next year's gala menu. Even if he'd moved on to a different hospital and city by then, he'd have a thick file to pass on to whoever took over after he left.

Aaron had just stuck a bite in his mouth when his gaze was drawn to the doorway. He nearly swallowed a shrimp whole when he saw the vision standing there.

She was tall and graceful, and the cascade of golden blond hair that had caught his eye the first time he'd seen her long ago was instead elegantly piled on top of her head. Wispy tendrils touched her cheeks and the long, slender curve of her neck. Her slim frame was accentuated by a long, pale blue dress that he would guess probably cost a tenth of what most of the women in this room had spent on their clothes, but she looked more gorgeous than any of them. Pretty much every time he'd passed by her in the hospital, he'd been struck by how amazingly good she managed to look in shapeless scrubs. But this woman?

This woman knocked his socks off.

He didn't know anything about her, except that she was one of the midwives at the hospital. He'd taken a second and third glance at her every time he'd seen her in a hallway, and who wouldn't? The woman was pure eye candy and obviously smart, too, but since his work didn't involve delivering the babies he helped parents create, he'd never had the pleasure of her acquaintance.

Maybe tonight was the night to change that. To tell her he was glad that at least a few of the midwives he'd invited had decided to come. To find out over a glass of champagne what adoption stories of patients whose babies she'd delivered she was planning to share with some of the donors. To casually see if there was a wedding ring on her finger...

He went to the lectern standing in front of a retractable screen that had been set up opposite the band to give his presentation. Applause met his speech and the slides he showed of the other Christmas party the foundation hosted each year, where children wanting a home met parents considering adoption. Then more pictures of happy families newly bonded together.

The nods of approval and glowing smiles around the room made him smile, too. A good sign that quite a few folks would give even more than the price their tickets had provided to the charity named after his adoptive parents, The Tom and Caroline Cartwright Foundation. When he was finished speaking he worked the crowd, shaking hands and answering questions.

The music started up again, and as people moved to the dance floor he took advantage of the break to grab a cold sparkling water. He scanned the crowd, hoping to catch another look at the beautiful blonde midwife and maybe introduce himself.

"Nice party you've got going here, Aaron."

He turned to see Sean Anderson standing next to him, holding a plate piled high with shrimp and crab cakes. The Aussie obstetrician had been at Cambridge Royal Maternity Unit for only a month or so, but Aaron had already seen the guy was both dedicated and talented.

"Thanks, but I can't take credit for all of it. Or any of it, if you ask my office manager. She spent months pulling this together."

"Deserving or not, take credit when you can. That's my motto." Sean grinned. "Even if you didn't plan the menu or send the invitations, I know you're the brains behind the whole idea, so kudos to you for that. Placing children with potential adoptive parents, especially older kids, is something anybody can get behind."

"I hope so. I also hope you and the other OBs will talk to folks about some of your patients who've found good homes for their babies, and parents who adopted. Those kinds of personal connections help a lot."

The man seemed to be looking past Aaron now, and when his response finally came, he sounded distracted. "Uh, yes. Will do."

Aaron looked over his shoulder and saw Isabel Delamere, another talented Australian OB. It didn't take much in the way of observation skills to see that her eyes met Sean's for a long moment. Her usual warm and friendly smile faded, and she turned away.

What was that all about? Sean hadn't been at CRMU long—surely he didn't have something going on with beautiful Isabel already? Could there be a professional rift between them? "You and Isabel have some kind of problem?"

"Problem?" Sean's attention came back to him slowly. "No, of course not."

But then it was Aaron's turn to be distracted as

the knock-out blonde midwife left the dance floor, leaving her dance partner with a smile before she moved toward the bar next to them.

"Hope!" Sean called out, and she turned. "Great job today on those twins."

She smiled and stepped closer to them. "Thank you, Dr. Anderson. They were both little peanuts, but I'm relieved they seem to be perfectly healthy."

Hope. So that was her name. It was the first time he'd been so close to the woman, and he couldn't help but stare. To notice that her eyes were a mesmerizing dark blue, her skin luminous, her lips full and rosy, and just looking at them made him decide right then and there that he wanted to kiss her.

"I don't think we've ever actually met," he said, holding out his hand. "I'm Aaron Cartwright."

Sean looked at him in surprise. "Sorry, I didn't realize. But of course, you probably haven't worked together. Aaron, this is Hope Sanders, a midwife at CRMU, and a darned good one. Hope, Dr. Aaron Cartwright. OB and fertility specialist."

"We may not have met, but I know who you

are, Dr. Cartwright. I've had more than one patient able to have the baby she's longed for, thanks to you." Her smile lit the room more than the glittering chandeliers as her slender hand shook his. "This is a wonderful party for a wonderful cause. Thanks so much for inviting us. I've already talked with a few donors about how your organization helps adoptive parents and children find one another."

"I appreciate that. I'm glad you were able to make it. Have you—"

"You know, I'll talk with you later, Aaron," Sean said, clapping Aaron on the shoulder. "I see someone I need to speak with. Congrats again on the crowd you've got here tonight."

He watched Sean move quickly across the room toward Isabel. He wondered again if they had something going, but whatever might be between them wasn't any of his business, and he had more interesting things to think about.

Like the very beautiful Hope Sanders.

"I think Sean and I interrupted your trek to the bar. Can I get you something?" He let his gaze roam over her face, fascinated by the exquisite shape of it, her silky brows, a pert nose above the delicately chiseled bow of her lip that tempted a man to explore its shape with his tongue.

"Just water, please. I was thirsty after dancing. The band you have here is fabulous, though I have to admit I'm a little surprised. Doesn't a party like this take a big chunk of the donations you're getting?"

"Seems like it would, doesn't it?" Interesting that she was tuned into that, when most people just enjoyed the extravaganza. "Some people donate generously simply because they understand the need. But I volunteered with a similar foundation in the States, and learned a lot that I've applied to this one. For better or worse, a great party with a high cost of admission has an exclusive aura to it. Foundations that spend big money on a fund-raising event like this reach people with the means to donate the most. They feel special, have a good time, and write checks."

"That seems...wrong."

"It's just human nature, which I know you understand well, working with patients all day." The little pucker over her eyes was cute as hell. "Think of it as a win-win. Everyone has a good time, and the foundation makes money to help families."

"I guess so." The pucker vanished as she smiled. "And I admit I'm having a very good time, so thank you again for inviting me."

"Glad you came." He tore his gaze from her appealing face, ratcheting back the libido that kept sending his thoughts places they shouldn't go with a woman he barely knew. "How about water with a glass of champagne on the side? In celebration of the party going off without a hitch."

"You do know saying something like that is tempting fate? The minute you're sure there's not a hitch, some disaster is sure to follow."

"You think?" Tempting fate? Her teasing smile was tempting all right, and who knew? Maybe fate was involved in that. Bringing her to this party so he could finally meet the woman who consistently grabbed his attention even from a distance.

"Dr. Cartwright. We just wanted to say you've put together another wonderful party."

He turned to the couple at his elbow and recognized them as big donors from last year. Spinning through his brain, he was relieved to come up with their names. "Mr. Adams. Mrs. Adams. Thank you, but my office manager organized it. I just show up. I'm glad you decided to come again this year."

"Wouldn't miss it," Mr. Adams said.

"Yes, we had a lovely time last Christmas and your foundation is doing such good things. We had a nice talk with Hope, here, who shared a few adoption stories that made us want to contribute even more. What a challenging job being a midwife must be."

"It can be," Hope said. "But of course it's tremendously rewarding to help bring new life into the world, and help the parents as well." She looked up at Aaron, and the admiration in her eyes surprised him. "Dr. Cartwright's work is both challenging and impressive. He helps parents have children who didn't think they could, and this wonderful foundation brings new families together in other ways."

Aaron nearly fidgeted under the admiring gazes of all three of them. It was the school of hard knocks, not heroism, that motivated the work he did.

"Well, we're very impressed with it," Mrs.

Adams said. "And now we're going to enjoy the decadent things on that dessert table."

After another handshake, they wandered off and Aaron turned to Hope. "Thanks for talking with them. Maybe you've veered onto the wrong career path, and sales and marketing are your real calling."

"Selling things I'm excited about? Easy. Selling itchy socks or bad-tasting toothpaste just because it was my job? I'm pretty sure I'd be an utter failure at that." The humor in her gaze, the sheer intelligence, drew him closer without even realizing he'd gone there.

He shoved his hands into his pockets, resisting a sudden urge to reach out and sweep away a tendril of hair that had slipped across her eye. Maybe she'd seen him staring at its silkiness, as her slender fingers lifted to her face, shoving it aside. Fingers that weren't wearing anything resembling a wedding ring.

And that knowledge kindled the hot spark of interest he'd felt the second she'd walked into the room. "I'd suggest again we share some champagne to eliminate all thoughts of bad-tasting toothpaste, but don't want to be pushy about drinking if you don't want to." Champagne was nice, but holding Hope Sanders close in his arms? An entire case of Dom Pérignon couldn't begin to compare to that kind of ambrosia. "So how about dancing with me instead?"

"Perhaps you haven't noticed they've just finished up a swing tune and aren't playing at the moment."

"That's funny, I hear music. Don't you?" That fate she'd talked about played right into his hand as a slow song began to echo around the room. She dazzled him with another smile as he reached for her hand, folding its soft warmth within his. He led her onto the floor, and the number of people crowding it made holding her fairly close a necessity he was more than happy about. "This kind of music is more my speed anyway, when it comes to dancing. Which for me mostly consists of rocking from one foot to the other, I'm sorry to say. Not my best talent."

"So what is your best talent?"

There was almost a seductive quality to her voice and the amazing blue of her eyes looking into his robbed him of breath. He was pretty sure she didn't realize the way she'd asked the question, and he fought down the desire to press her body even closer to his, along with an offer to show her one of them.

"Hmm, that's a tough one. I'm good at my job, but I'm not sure that qualifies as a talent. I can kick a mean soccer ball and used to throw a damn good football spiral, too." He lowered his head close to her ear, and her soft hair tickled his temple. "But probably my best talent?"

"I think I'm sorry I asked." Her voice was a little breathy, and the sexy sound of it sent him sliding his palm from between her shoulder blades down to just above the curve of her shapely behind, bringing her body closer to his.

"Sorry, why?"

"Afraid that maybe your talent is something my innocent ears can't handle."

"Are your ears innocent?" He studied her, amused and curious. Innocent, no, as she clearly was used to sophisticated banter. But there was something guileless about her, a sweetness and sincerity that went beyond appealing. "Don't worry, I'm a gentleman. Your ears are safe."

Their bodies swaying together in a fit so perfect it was hard to tell where his body began and hers ended, they danced in silence for long minutes. Her sweet scent filled his nose, and he closed his eyes and breathed her in, holding her close enough to feel the brush of her breasts against his chest. Her forehead grazed his chin and her hand was tucked into his and pressed to his sternum as if they knew each other much better than two people who had met only ten minutes ago.

Aaron had been with quite a few women in his life, and he found himself studying the curve of her ear, the smoothness of her skin, trying to figure out what, exactly, made this feel somehow different. Had he ever felt a connection this instant and intense with anyone before? Or was he just not remembering?

The music drew to a close and they slowly separated, their eyes meeting. Her lips were parted, her skin seemed a little flushed, and it took every ounce of willpower for Aaron to remember they were in a public place in the middle of a hundred people. To remember he couldn't pull her back into his arms and kiss her until neither of them could breathe.

"You still haven't told me," Hope said, apparently trying to bring normalcy back to the moment, replacing the chemistry that was pinging hot and fast between them.

"Told you what?"

"What your best talent is."

Damn if the curve of her lips wasn't pure temptation. Temptation to try to impress her by showing her at least one answer to that question.

CHAPTER TWO

HOPE'S HEART KEPT doing an uncontrollable little dance of its own as she looked up at Aaron Cartwright. At the smile in his rich brown eyes as they stared into hers. She wasn't sure what had prompted her to ask that question. Again. She might not be a shy belle, but neither was she a flirtatious siren. Yet here she was, saying things that couldn't be interpreted as anything but suggestive.

She'd hoped she might meet Aaron at this party. But she hadn't expected to dance with the tall, ridiculously good-looking fertility specialist that practically every nurse and midwife at the hospital swooned over when he passed through the hallways.

She'd never have dreamed it possible, but the man was even more swoon-worthy in his tuxedo. And here she was, being held in his strong arms, dancing so closely they could have kissed by moving their faces barely an inch.

His deliciously male body radiating heat like a furnace, the way his big hand caught and held hers against his muscular chest, the deep, sexy rumble of his voice in her ear, all had combined to steal every molecule of breath from her lungs and, apparently, all sense from her brain as well. How else could she explain asking him—a second time, as though she really needed to know—what his best talent was?

Lord. She swallowed, embarrassment seeping through her body, adding to the heat that had nearly sent her up in flames. She stepped off the dance floor with him fluidly moving next to her and opened her mouth to say something, anything, that could possibly make him forget her last question, when he spoke.

"Punting."

She stared up at him blankly. "Punting?"

"Maybe not my best talent, but yes, I'm very good at it."

A nervous and relieved laugh escaped her throat. Thank heavens he wasn't going to take her up on her unfortunate innuendo. "You already told me you're good at kicking a football… er…soccer ball to Americans. Unless you mean gambling?"

"I never gamble. At least, not with money." He slid her a teasing look, and the way his eyes crinkled at the corners messed with her breathing all over again. "The punting I'm referring to is in a boat. You may think only Cambridge residents and tourists enjoy lazily shoving themselves down a river, but we've been doing it back home for centuries, too."

"And where is back home?" Since the midwives liked to talk about the various handsome men in the hospital, she knew he was American and from California, but not much other than that.

"Northern California. Wine country."

"Wine country? And here I'd assumed being from California that you were a surfer dude."

His eyes twinkled as the crinkles around them got deeper. "I've surfed, but I don't think that moniker fits me. And do you have any idea how adorable the words 'surfer dude' sound in your wonderful British accent?"

"I don't have an accent. You're the one with an accent." Which she found incredibly sexy, she had to admit, but wasn't about to say that and embarrass herself all over again.

"If you say so." He leaned closer. "But please let me hear you say 'surfer dude' one more time."

She laughed and felt her face heat again, but this time she had a feeling it was from his closeness, and how wonderful he smelled and looked, and how it all made her heart beat a little faster. "So people punt in wine country? Are there little canals between the vineyards?" she joked.

"Yes. They're filled with grape juice." His wink and grin were so charming, she had a bad feeling she might swoon for real next time she saw him at the hospital, requiring a hefty dose of smelling salts. "The punting I did back home was in Denver, Colorado, where I went to med school. Learned on Cherry Creek, and eventually raced. All the punting here is one of the reasons I liked the idea of working in Cambridge for a while."

"I find it hard to believe you consider punting a talent. I mean, how difficult could it be to shove a boat down a river with a pole?"

"You live here and don't know the answer to that?" He stared at her. "Punting takes a lot of practice. And it's excellent exercise. Surely you've tried it?"

"Well, no actually. I've been on the River Cam many times in the punts, but always had someone else manning the pole. Should I be embarrassed to admit that, since I was born and raised here?"

"This is shocking. And also unacceptable." He shook his head as his warm palm slid down her arm to grasp her elbow, propelling her across the room. "I assume you have a coat checked?"

"Yes, but—"

"Do you have a car here?"

"No, I came with another midwife from the hospital. I—"

"Good." They stopped at the coat check closet and he held out his hand. "May I have your ticket?"

She fumbled in her evening bag for it, wondering what in the world he was up to, and why she was getting out the ticket and giving it to him when she had no idea as to the answer. "The party's only half over. Are you throwing me out because I'm a shame to the CRMU and the entire city of Cambridge?"

He flashed her a devastating smile. "You, Hope

Sanders, are obviously a shining star. Which is also why we have to fix this problem immediately. I'm taking you to the River Cam for a little punting lesson."

"What? Surely you can't leave this early? Besides, it's freezing outside! I can't believe you did your punting in November."

"I can leave whenever I want. I've given my talk and the guests are all happy. And it's not freezing." He slid her coat on before donning his own. "Fifty degrees Fahrenheit is downright balmy. We punted year round, just like people do here, in much colder temps than that."

"But I'm wearing a long gown! And you're in a tuxedo, for heaven's sake." Was the man out of his mind? No way was she getting on that river tonight, but she couldn't deny feeling a thrill of excitement at the idea of going out with Aaron Cartwright. Which was utterly crazy, since now was definitely not the time to get involved with a man. Not with her life about to change forever. "I'm not punting tonight and that's that."

"I'm about to gamble that you might change your mind about that, Ms. Sanders. Let's hit a pub by the river and decide from there." The humor in his eyes and the feel of his warm hand closing around hers left her with zero ability to protest again. "Come on."

Hope was still a little disbelieving that she was now sitting intimately close to Aaron Cartwright as he drove his purring sports car through the city. They talked about the hospital and work, but the bland conversation didn't slow her heart rate to normal. Probably because he smelled amazingly good, looked even better and kept glancing at her with unmistakable interest in his eyes.

No use in pretending to herself that she didn't share that interest. But from what she'd heard, the man was one of those love-'em-and-leave-'em types, involved with a woman for just a few months before moving on. Of course, her own history had proven she wasn't relationship material anyway. Not to mention that, scary though it was, she was about to give herself the gift of a child very soon. The child she'd dreamed of forever.

Since neither one of them was into relationships, this odd excursion wasn't a big deal, then, right? Why not just go along for the ride and enjoy herself?

He parked the car, then walked around the front of it to open her door. The moment she stepped out, a chilly wind whipped her hair, dipped inside her coat collar and fluttered the skirt of her dress. She hugged herself and cocked her head at him. "Still think it's downright balmy out here?"

"Maybe it's not quite as balmy as I thought." He wrapped his long arm around her shoulders and pulled her against his side as they walked to the path lining the river. The glow of electric lamps warmly illuminated the stony path and the dark water as it flowed hypnotically beside them. The brick exteriors of several pubs were lit, too, as they strolled past rows of empty punts bobbing shoulder to shoulder in the water. "A glass of brandy might warm us up, then we'll decide if maybe this was a harebrained idea after all."

"No maybe about it." Then again, without his harebrained idea, she wouldn't be standing here in the curve of his arm being held close to his big, warm body, which felt absurdly cozy and nice. "But I admit it's beautiful outside tonight.

And I also hate to admit that I rarely come here to enjoy it."

"Too busy working? Or playing?"

"Working." She was past her playing days. Though at that moment, the pleasure she felt just walking with Aaron in the crisp, starry night made her wonder if that was as true as she'd believed it was.

The thought brought her to a sudden standstill. Of course she was done with her playing days. Hadn't wanted them for years anyway. She'd gone out on the town because there'd been no one special in her life, and no child of her own to keep her home. Enjoying this night out with Aaron didn't mean she wasn't capable of being a loving, dedicated mother.

She glanced up at Aaron and could tell he wondered why she'd stopped walking. She forced a smile at him and started moving again. "Plus, I live on the outskirts of town, so I just don't get into the city center very often."

"You said you were born and raised here?"

"Yes. Been here forever. Went to university here, too, except when I did my advanced midwife training in London." He was looking at her a little quizzically. "I take it you think that's a little strange, since you lived in California, went to university in Denver and now you're here."

"I've traveled to a lot of other places over the years. Been accused many times of being the stone that refuses to gather moss." His teeth flashed in a white smile. "I don't think it's strange that you've dug roots in here, but I admit moving around is more my style. That I've been here three years is a surprise to me, to be honest. I'm sure the travel bug will bite me one of these days and I'll move on."

The utter opposite of Hope. She couldn't imagine how he didn't feel a need to put down roots somewhere. Cambridge felt like a part of her, deeply entwined with her heart and her soul, and settling in there forever like a broody hen with her job and a family was all she'd ever wanted.

The patio of the pub they came to held a few hardy souls sitting at a table, but most were cozy inside. Cheerful music somehow penetrated beyond the thick brick to where they stood, and through the windows Hope could see a crowd of people mingling and laughing. Those days would be completely behind her very soon, and she closed her eyes and smiled, visualizing her new future.

Motherhood.

Despite the chill, she wasn't ready to go inside. She wanted to breathe in the fresh air and take in the surprising pleasure of walking with a man holding her close before there would be no possibility of that happening anytime soon.

She looked up at Aaron, surprised to see his eyes were on her and not the pub, his expression inscrutable. "Shall we walk just a bit farther?" she asked, wanting the moment to last a little longer. "That bridge up ahead is spectacular."

"The whole city is beautiful. I've been impressed with its architecture since the day I got here." He tugged her closer as they resumed their walk. "The path ends at the bridge, so we'll have to double back or climb the stairs from the riverbank to the restaurants and pubs up there."

The glow of lights faded behind them as they neared the dead end just before the old gothic-style bridge, where one lone punt disappeared on the water beyond it. Aaron dropped his arm from her shoulders, sliding it down to grasp her hand again as he turned to look at her. "I enjoy walking along here often," he said, his voice quiet. "But tonight it's especially beautiful. Thanks for coming with me, even though you didn't really want to."

"It was punting in an evening dress that was the problem, Dr. Cartwright. And the cold air. And the threat of exercise." Though she wasn't feeling at all cold. In fact, an intense warmth seemed to be creeping across every inch of her skin beneath her coat. "Who knew I'd be glad you dragged me here?"

He laughed, the sound a soft rumble in his chest as he drew her close. "So my gamble paid off." Then he lowered his mouth to hers.

For one split second, she was stunned with surprise. Then it was quickly gone, replaced by a punch of desire the likes of which she hadn't felt for a long, long time. Her eyelids flickered closed as his mouth moved oh-so-skillfully on hers. Teasing and tasting, sweet then intense, with a hunger that made her dizzy. She gasped into his mouth as her heart pounded and her knees wobbled, and she blindly lifted her hands to grip his wide shoulders so she wouldn't sink straight to the stone path.

His mouth moved from hers to caress the sensitive spot beneath her ear before warmly sliding across her jawline and up her cold cheek to rest at the corner of her lips. "You taste better than anything on that buffet dessert table, Hope," he whispered. "Better than champagne. Better than the finest vintage in Napa Valley."

"Have you had every fine vintage in Napa?" she breathed.

"No." She could feel him smile against her mouth. "Not necessary to know with absolute certainty that it's true, though I've had my share."

His share of wine or his share of women? Women for sure, if rumor was to be believed. And she did believe, because there was no doubt other women found him as completely irresistible as she did, considering she'd barely spent an hour with the man and was kissing him as she hadn't kissed anyone in pretty much forever.

His mouth covered hers again in another kiss that left her quivering. When their lips finally separated, quick breaths came hard and fast against each other's cold skin.

Moonlight gleamed on his dark brown hair, creating shadows beneath his prominent cheekbones and highlighting a stubborn jaw. His brown eyes no longer seemed warmly chocolatey, but instead glittered like molten onyx, hot and dangerous. Her insides quivered and she tried to think of something to say, but couldn't come up with a single, rational thought.

"I've decided you were right," he said in a low voice.

"Right?"

"About punting tonight. Staying inside where it's warm and showing you another of my talents is a much better idea."

That startled a laugh out of her. "Mmm-hmm. And I can guess what those talents might be, Dr. Has-A-Big-Ego. I can also guess that showing me those talents was your plan all along."

"Plan, no. But hoping to get to know the beautiful Hope I've noticed so often in the hospital? That I'm delighted to learn is single?" His hand slipped down to grasp hers, his thumb stroking across her empty ring finger. "Oh, yeah. I freely admit I'd hoped for that."

"That's a lot of hope in one sentence," she said, trying for a little humor so she could catch her breath and banish thoughts of those talents he boasted, which, based on his amazing kissing skills, she was more than ready to believe on a scale of one to ten were probably a twenty.

As for being single, that was true. The way she was wired, apparently. Something sadly missing in her DNA. The other reason she wasn't really available despite her single status would doubtless surprise him. Maybe even shock him.

"I guess it is. But one thing I never thought to hope for is this unbelievable chemistry between us. Unless it's only me who feels like a nuclear bomb just went off in my head from kissing you. Is it?"

She stared into the gaze searching hers, the question hanging in their dark depths. She opened her mouth to answer, but found her throat all closed up at the heat she saw there, at the dangerous current swirling around as if the two of them were standing in some electrified tornado.

"Is it, Hope?"

Her name on his lips, spoken in a deep voice that promised a delicious pleasure she hadn't had in so long, and definitely wouldn't have for even longer, maybe even ever, sent her closing the gap between them. Shocking her. Speaking her surprising answer against his lips. "No. It's not just you."

The kiss was excruciatingly soft and sweet and went on so long, she felt dizzy. When their lips separated, they just stared at one another until he spoke in a rough voice.

"I live just a block away." His warm lips pressed softly against one chilled cheek, then the other. Feathered against each eyelid before his gaze met hers again. "I want you, which I'm sure doesn't come as a surprise. Will you come home with me to see where our undeniable chemistry leads? And if you decide it leads to just a glass of wine or brandy, that's okay."

Oh. My. God. He wanted her. The sexy man she'd have to confess she'd had more than one fantasy about wanted *her*.

Not that she was completely taken aback, after his comment about nuclear explosions and those knee-melting kisses they'd shared. And after hearing the stories of his lifestyle. Her heart pounded so hard in her chest, she was sure he could probably hear it.

Did she really want to be another notch in his bedpost?

Her gaze took in how his dark hair blew across his forehead, how his lips were curved in a small smile, how his brown eyes gleamed with an unmistakable desire and, for the first time in her life, she wanted to say *Oh, yes!* to a one-night fling.

As she looked at him she thought about her new life right there on the horizon. A new life which would be all about changes to her body and sleepless nights and new responsibilities. Didn't she pride herself on knowing what she wanted and making it happen? What would be wrong with enjoying one, doubtless delectable night with Aaron Cartwright? She never worked with the man, and a one-night fling wasn't any kind of real relationship anyway, right?

"I…um…" She licked her lips and tried again. "I'm not in a place in my life where I want a relationship."

"I'm never in a place in my life where I want a relationship." His smile widened. "At least not one that's long-term. I don't stay put in one place long enough for that. But time with you, getting to know all about Hope Sanders and who she is and what she likes? That I'd like very much."

His hand dropped hers to cup her cheek, warm

against her cool skin, and his thumb slipped across her cheekbone with the same feathery touch he'd used on her fingers. Hope quivered as her thoughts suddenly turned to how those fingers might feel against other parts of her body.

"I meant I'm not in a place where we could spend any time together other than tonight."

"Other than tonight?" His dark brows raised slightly, his eyes now looking both perplexed and slightly amused. "Got to say, a woman saying she wants to kick me out the door after one night together is a first."

"Wouldn't be kicking you out, because it's your own house." She managed a breathless laugh. "I admit it's a first for me, too. But that's all I can offer and…and…"

As she struggled to figure out what to say he touched his lips gently to hers. "And what?"

"And I'm offering it." She gulped in disbelief that the words had actually come out of her mouth. But as his lips sweetly, softly pressed against hers, warm and tender and oh-so-delicious, her disbelief and uncertainty faded. She lifted her hands to the sides of his strong neck as heat radiated from him, warming her even through her coat. It all felt so good, so wonderful, so right, she knew she wouldn't regret being with him tonight. Just one evening of excitement and passion with a strong, sexy man before everything in her life changed.

He pulled back, and the eyes staring into hers were that smoldering, dark onyx again. "You might not believe it, but I'm not normally a one-night-stand guy. If that's all you're willing to offer, though, I find it's damned impossible for me to say no. We'll go to my apartment and have that nightcap, and you can decide then where, if anywhere, you'd like the rest of the evening to go before I take you home."

His hand wrapped around hers again, and he led her up the stone steps. He was moving fast, and she nearly tripped in her heels. He looked at her feet and slowed down as his hot gaze lifted to hers again. "Sorry. I forgot you had those things on. Very sexy," he said, leaning down to brush his warm lips against her cheek. "But not so great for walking, hmm? Thankfully, we don't have to go far."

They didn't speak again on the short trek, and Hope's breath was short, but not from the walk. Her chest was filled with a crazy excitement that completely overwhelmed the nervous butterflies in her stomach.

They trotted up short steps to a gorgeous Victorian-style stone building with two ornate front doors, and Hope had to pause to admire it.

"Is this a semi? Do you own this one side?"

"Yes, it's a duplex and my neighbor is a nice, quiet, older lady. But since I move around a lot, renting is always the way to go."

Apparently it was true that the man wanted nothing to tie him down, but it wasn't any of her business why he felt that way. His hand palmed her back as she stepped inside the door on the right, the butterflies now flapping a little more insistently. He shut the door behind them, and his eyes met hers for the briefest moment before he wrapped his arms around her, pulled her close and kissed her.

There was nothing sweet or gentle or teasing about this one. It went from zero to sixty in a split second, hot and intense, his tongue exploring her mouth with a thoroughness that weakened her knees and melted every brain cell. She let her hands slip up his chest and the sides of his neck into his soft thick hair, mussing it even more than the breeze had, and found herself pressing his mouth somehow even closer to hers, deepening the kiss until she was quivering from head to toe.

"I keep my home pretty chilly. But kissing you has definitely warmed me up." The dark hunger in his eyes as he pulled back made it hard to breathe. Even harder when he reached to flick her coat buttons open one by one. He tossed the coat on a chair behind him, then took off his own. "You warmer now, too? Would you like that brandy we talked about? Or a glass of wine?"

His voice was husky, and Hope was surprised at the sincerity in it, considering the gleam in his eyes and the shortness of his breath that mirrored her own. He clearly had truly meant what he'd said about giving her time to decide what she wanted from the evening. It added one more layer to his already delicious appeal, and every last vestige of doubt slid away as she tugged at the bow of his tie until it lay loose around his neck.

"Would you be surprised if I told you that every time I saw you at the hospital, fantasies of kissing you and being with you usually followed? So even though we don't really know each other, somehow I feel like we do. Like those fantasies were real." It was true, and she was surprised she didn't feel embarrassed to tell him. To help him understand why she felt good about being here with him tonight. "So right now I don't want a drink. What I want is for those fantasies to truly become real."

His gaze slid to her mouth, to the beading on her dress above her breasts, before slowly meeting hers again. "You can be sure you've starred in my fantasies as well, Hope Sanders. I always assumed a woman like you would already be taken by some lucky guy, and I'm more than glad to learn that's not the case." His lips tilted in a slow smile. "But I know it must be because you dump all the men eager to be with you as soon as you've had your way with them."

That hadn't been her failing, but she was glad he didn't know what was. "Not quite accurate, but I'm finding it rather fun to pretend to be that woman tonight."

He grasped her shoulders and turned her around. Cool air swept her hot skin as he tugged on the tab of her zipper, his soft, moist mouth pressing against the side of her neck.

His lips crept along her skin as he lowered the

zipper inch by inch, his hands trailing after in a slow, shivery path so heart-poundingly delicious she feared she might pass out from the intense pleasure of it. Over her shoulder blade, her spine, sliding the dress off as he went, ending with his hands grasping her hips and his tongue caressing the indentations above each buttock.

"Your skin feels so soft," he whispered. "Tastes so good."

Trembling, she could have stood there for ever savoring the feel of his hands and mouth, the rumble of his low voice against her flesh. Except she didn't want to be the only one standing there half-naked, and she turned. Trembling even more when she realized he'd crouched down to kiss her back, and that his mouth was now just above her panties. Slowly, excruciatingly, kissing all across the lacy top before lazily licking her skin beneath.

Part of her wanted him to just keep going with all the licking and kissing that was short-circuiting all thoughts except how incredibly good it felt. But the part of her brain that somehow still worked had her grasping his arms to tug him upright before she just lay down on the floor and begged him to make love to her.

"Not fair for me to be standing here freezing while you're still dressed." Though freezing was about the last word to describe how she really felt. "I'd undo your shirt, except I don't know what to do with those little pearl buttons."

"I'm perfectly happy with things staying unfair, but if you insist."

He stood to tower over her—something she wasn't used to at five feet eight inches. "How tall are you, anyway?" she asked absently, staring with fascination as his fingers flicked open his buttons one by one, slowly revealing dark brown hair in the center of his chest that tapered down to a taut stomach.

"Six foot three or so."

His shirt slipped off him completely, showing smooth, broad shoulders and a torso that was thickly muscled and masculine and so sexy, her mouth watered. She'd thought the man swoon-worthy in a suit and tie, scrubs, or tux. None of that had prepared her for the sheer, male beauty that was Aaron Cartwright.

Speechless, she stared at him as he kicked off his shoes and tossed his belt on the floor. The brown eyes that met hers glittered with the same crazy desire she felt, but he had that appealing little smile on his lips, too, as he wrapped one arm around her and kissed her. Without the intensity of the deep kiss they'd shared the minute they'd stepped inside his door. This one was sweet, and slow, tasting like a promise, and she couldn't help but melt right into him. The kiss stayed mind-blowingly tender as his fingers moved to trace the lace of her bra, then slipped inside to caress her nipple. It felt so good, so wonderful, she moved back a smidge to give him better access.

"I guess...this is that talent you were talking about," she managed to whisper as they kissed. "You weren't lying about being good at it."

"Did I say I wanted to show you just one talent?" She felt him smile against her mouth. "I have more."

She smiled, too, since, holy wow, that was beyond true. His kisses and caresses were pretty much the best things she'd enjoyed in forever. "Does that big ego count as a talent?"

"No." His fingers moved to trace where his tongue had gone inside the lace of her panties, and her amusement faded with a gasp as they moved south to stroke her moist folds. "My big ego is a failing of mine, so if you can help me with doing better, I'd appreciate it."

She bit back a moan. "Having an orgasm right this second probably wouldn't help you with that."

"No. But it would make me very happy." His hot breath mingled with hers as their tongues continued a gentle dance. The feel of the hard muscle of his chest with its soft hair beneath her hands, his low voice, and the excruciatingly wonderful touch of his fingers expertly moving on her most sensitive part sent her over the edge she hadn't wanted to go over, and she shuddered and moaned.

"I didn't mean for that to happen." Gasping, she slumped against him feeling slightly embarrassed. But mostly she felt incredibly, amazingly, quiveringly good. From just his touch and nothing else.

He held her tightly against him, and his hand slipped from her wetness to cup her rear inside her panties. His lips touched her cheek, her ear, her forehead. "I did." His voice sounded breathless, too, and rough, and also very satisfied, damn it.

"I guess I failed in my assignment to help keep that ego of yours in check."

"I'm probably a hopeless case, anyway." He chuckled as his lips pressed the corner of her mouth. "Let's go somewhere more comfortable, hmm?"

She didn't care where they went, so long as it was for more of the bliss he'd just given her. The floor would be fine with her, but he led her to a room with a big, wide bed. He yanked back the covers before he picked her up and deposited her into the middle of it. He stared at her, and the fire in his eyes scorched every inch of her body they perused, making her tremble all over again. Had any man ever looked at her like that before?

"You are a beautiful woman, Hope." He yanked off his trousers and socks and she had a heart-stopping moment to admire his gorgeous naked-ness and the clear evidence that he was every bit as aroused as she was. "Even more beautiful than my fantasies."

"My fantasies about you had you being pretty godlike, Dr. Cartwright. And let me say you've met those expectations quite well. Except, oops, there I go forgetting about that ego assignment again."

Another chuckle rumbled from his chest into hers as he lay next to her on the bed and pulled her close, kissing her and touching her until she'd have been hard pressed to come up with her own name. Dimly, she realized her underwear was now off and every inch of her body was quivering from the touch of his mouth and talented fingers. She tried to return the favor as much as she possibly could in the state of sexual intoxication he'd driven her to, but found every sense focused on the intense pleasure he was giving her.

Finally, he rose above her and sheathed himself with a condom before he slid inside her more-than-ready body. Their eyes met and held in a spellbinding connection she couldn't remember ever experiencing while making love with a man. They moved together, their bodies fitting perfectly just as they had at the dance. Even as Hope absorbed the rhythmic pleasure of it all, the feel of his skin against hers, the look in his eyes and the taste of his mouth, the foggy edge of her mind was aware of a twinge of regret that they could share this moment only once. Aware of a sense of confusion over how all this couldn't be new to her experience, and yet it was.

But there was one thing she wasn't confused about. Once was far, far better than never.

CHAPTER THREE

AARON HEADED DOWN the hospital corridor to begin his first procedure of the day and stopped dead when he glimpsed a tall, slender woman dressed in scrubs walking toward one of the labor suites at the end of the hall. A tidy ponytail tamed the silky golden hair he could still feel tickling his skin as it had loosened from its elegant knot, and her face in profile reminded him of a stunning, alabaster cameo of a goddess.

Hope Sanders.

His heart kicked hard in his chest and he stood stock still, mesmerized by the smile she gave a nurse as she paused outside the door. A smile so dazzling it had seemed to light the entire ballroom the moment she'd directed it at him, making him smile back and want another one. A smile that had changed from interestingly intelligent, to fun and flirty, to filled with a deeply sensuous bliss he'd been incredibly lucky to put there.

Damn. He realized his breath was a little fast, and his heart rate, too, and it was a good thing she disappeared into the labor suite or he might have found his feet heading her way before he'd even thought about it.

The attraction he'd felt for her before, just from seeing her in the hospital, was nothing compared to the attraction he felt now that he knew a little more about how smart and charming she was. How good she tasted, how soft her skin felt, how beautiful every inch of her body was. How well her body fit his, and how he hadn't been able to stop thinking about all that since the moment he'd kissed her goodbye.

That kiss had been sweet and hot and intense like all the others they'd shared. A kiss that had felt as if it held plenty of promise, until she'd broken it and taken a step back and he'd known the promise wasn't there at all. Something about the look on her face at that moment had shown she wanted to bring a distance between them that wasn't just physical. A determined look that said she'd meant it when she'd stated there was no possibility of them spending any more time together, and he had to wonder why.

Also wonder if, maybe, he could convince her otherwise.

Or maybe karma was catching up with him, and he was getting served with the "it's been fun but gotta run" that he'd ended relationships with many a time. Except she wanted to end this one a whole lot sooner than he'd ever done. He knew he should just enjoy the memory of their one night and move on. He also knew he damn well couldn't forget all about Hope Sanders, even though she'd said and shown loud and clear that he had no choice about it.

Could all these unsettling feelings be a sign he'd been in Cambridge long enough? A sign that it was time to move on? He didn't want or need to get entwined with any one woman or any one place. Maybe he should start thinking of where in the world he'd like to live next.

With that thought, he went into the procedure room to see his patients, John and Angela Walters. Resolutely refocusing his attention on his job and what they all hoped to achieve.

"Good morning," Aaron said as he sat in front of Angela. "The big day is here. Are you two ready?"

"More than ready, Dr. Cartwright. You know we've been waiting for this for a long time," John said through his surgical mask, reaching to grip his wife's hand as she lay in the hospital bed, gowned and ready. While they were understandably on edge, the couple seemed slightly more relaxed than they had been in his office last Friday, and Aaron was glad to see it. Hopefully that meant they'd listened to all he'd talked to them about and had read the extra literature. Knew the risks, and also that the odds were in their favor for achieving what they hoped for, which was a successful pregnancy and healthy baby.

"Dr. Miller told me your part went well, John." Next came a little light humor, which always helped everyone relax. "I hope it wasn't miserable—Dr. Miller and I both dread being on people's hate list. Makes it hard to sleep."

"Guess your sleep is safe enough," John said, his eyes smiling over his mask. "Not something I want to do every day, but it wasn't too terrible."

"Glad to hear it. And we shouldn't have to do it again, even if we need to try the ICSI once more. Freezing the fertilized embryos in case we need them will make things easier next time, though I have every hope that won't be necessary."

"I still can't believe freezing doesn't hurt them, Dr. Cartwright," Angela said, the anxious look forming on her face again.

"It is a little hard to imagine, isn't it? But they're still really just cells at that point so it's true, I promise."

"I, um, know I already said this." Angela nervously licked her lips, and Aaron prepared himself for whatever misgivings she might be having. "But I'm worried about implanting only two eggs. We've been through so much, and I know John and I can handle multiples, if that should happen."

"Two implanted eggs should result in a baby," he said, trying to keep his voice gentle and understanding, but it was an effort to battle down his frustration. If only would-be parents fully believed and understood the challenges he tried to educate them about. The kinds of challenges and terrible consequences that the stress of multiple births sometimes put parents through.

Your mother just couldn't handle so many babies on her own, Aaron. I'm sorry we came all this way and she didn't want to see you. But ev-

eryone's hoping she can get better and leave the hospital sometime soon. We'll visit another time, okay? Maybe she'll want to see you then.

Aaron squeezed his eyes shut for a second, willing away the unwelcome memory of one of his foster parents' words. One foster parent out of several, whose names he couldn't remember anymore. One of many memories, some the same, some different, but always disturbing. Always painful. Hating that they invaded his brain when he least wanted them.

He opened his eyes to focus on Angela, somehow giving her a smile. Forcing his voice to a lighter tone. "A woman isn't a Golden Retriever, you know. Your very human uterus wasn't designed to carry a litter of pups, was it?"

"Okay, point taken." Aaron was relieved to see her smile, glad it wasn't going to become an issue just before the procedure was to begin. "I never thought I'd say this to anyone except John, but— are you ready to make a baby?"

"Oh, yeah, I'm ready," Aaron said. They all chuckled, and he looked around for the nurse to get this show on the road. The quicker they got Angela sedated and her eggs retrieved, the better.

Except only the ultrasound technician and the patient care specialist were there, not his nurse. "Where's Kathy?"

"I don't know, Doctor. She hasn't been here since I brought the Walters in."

Strange. Kathy was as reliable as an atomic clock. "Would you mind finding her? I—"

"Dr. Cartwright." A nurse poked her head through the doorway. "Wanted to let you know Kathy's come down with a nasty bug, and she's had to go home."

"Can you assist me, then?"

"Sorry." Her face twisted in apology. "I'm helping one of the midwives with a delivery. And baby's coming soon so I need to get back in there."

"All right. Thanks." Well, damn. He pulled down his mask to give another reassuring smile to the couple. "Sorry, but you'll have to hang on just a few more minutes. I'll find a nurse and be right back."

He strode toward the labor and delivery suite, figuring he could find a midwife whose patient wouldn't be delivering for a while, and who would be quite safe in the hands of the midwife's assistant until later. Refusing to admit that the assistant he really wanted to find had long blonde hair and sweet lips and a body that was beyond seductive, even in shapeless green scrubs.

Then, as though he'd willed it, the woman on his mind stepped out of the doorway he'd seen her go into not much earlier.

"Hope." He picked up the pace until he stood next to her. Close enough to see the fascinating green and black flecks within the blue of her eyes. "I'm about to retrieve a patient's eggs, then do ICSI, except my nurse has gone home sick. Any chance you're free to assist?"

"Assist?" Her blue eyes stared up at him, and the zing that had happened the second he'd met her at the party crackled the air between them. Against his will, he found his gaze dropping to her full pink lips as she licked them. Nervously? Because she felt the same electric current he did?

He couldn't help but smile at that thought, but the hospital corridor wasn't exactly the place to see where all that electricity might lead, since he was pretty sure it would be similar to a high-voltage lightning strike like before. He schooled his expression into a professional cool. "Yes. I'll need you to do an IV sedation and monitor her as I retrieve the eggs. Should only take about ten minutes. Twenty tops."

"All right." Her face relaxed into a smile. "I've never seen this procedure, so it should be interesting."

"Good. The patient is a little nervous, so I appreciate your helping before she gets too worried."

As he'd expected, Mr. and Mrs. Walters were looking anxious again. "Nurse Midwife Hope Sanders is here to help, Angela. Hope, this is Angela and John Walters. Right after we retrieve the eggs, I'm going to do the ICSI procedure to fertilize them and see which ones want to develop into a baby."

"Thank you for coming, Hope." Angela was gripping her husband's hand like a lifeline. "We were getting worried we'd have to wait until another time, and that would be torture."

"I'm happy to help," Hope said, her smile friendly and sincere as she scrubbed and put on a gown and mask. "The CRMU prides itself on avoiding patient torture whenever possible."

The couple chuckled, and Aaron marveled at

how easily she put them at ease—much more easily than he'd managed to do. "Time for you to go to sleep for a little while, Angela. Hope, will you please get her IV sedation going?"

Aaron watched her place the IV in Angela's arm, impressed at how quickly and painlessly she had it ready. The woman was obviously an excellent nurse, which didn't surprise him. He'd bet she was a great midwife, too, chatting with birthing mothers in the same soothing tone she was using with Angela, having the woman more relaxed than he'd ever seen her.

"Nicely done, Hope. Obviously an expert."

Her eyes smiled at him over her mask before she administered the drug and in moments the patient was sedated. The ultrasound tech placed the monitor just above Angela's pelvis to give Aaron a good picture of her ovaries.

"John, you're welcome to stay, but it may make you uncomfortable to watch. If you decide you want to wait outside, we all completely understand and will take good care of Angela."

John nodded, and the way his face paled just from the ultrasound told Aaron the man would probably have to leave when the needle was inserted to retrieve his wife's eggs. He knew the man wanted to be there though, and tried to distract him by explaining what was going on, to keep his attention on the monitor instead of the needle that tended to freak out husbands.

"Watch the monitor, John," he said as he worked. "You're looking at Angela's ovary. We've got some good-sized follicles here, which should give us a nice number of eggs."

"Yes. Good."

Aaron glanced at John, who'd gone a pasty gray and was leaning a little sideways in his chair. He sent a quick look to the patient care specialist and nodded toward John before turning his attention back to the monitor again. "Don't want you to pass out, John. How about going out to the waiting room? We'll be done here in no time, then you can come back to support Angela when she wakes up. Okay?"

The patient care specialist had obviously gotten the hint and was already taking John's arm and leading him from the room. As Aaron studied the monitor while he worked he was aware of Hope intently watching the procedure.

"Glad you noticed he wasn't looking too well.

I was about to say the exact same thing, though it wouldn't really have been my place to do that."

"Keeping someone from fainting and cracking their head open on the floor is anyone's job." Their eyes met, and being able to just see her eyes and not the rest of her pretty face made him notice how long her lashes were. How expressive her gaze was.

"How many eggs do you usually get?" she asked.

"Eight to ten is a good number, but the number might be a lot smaller if the woman is older. Angela thankfully has quite a few eggs, considering she's going on forty. Shouldn't have any problem getting some very viable ones."

"That's good news for them, I assume?"

"Hopefully. But the next part of the equation might be the trickiest one."

"What part?"

Since she was a member of the medical team helping with the procedure, it was perfectly ethical to share their history with her, and he explained the details of the ICSI procedure.

She nodded, a thoughtful crease between her

brows as she stared at the monitor. "So what happens now?"

"In just a few more minutes, I'll be done retrieving the fluid and eggs, then they'll be sent to the IVF lab. They'll be rinsed in a culture media and put in a dish for about four hours, then they'll be ready for fertilization. I'll study the eggs to see which look the most viable and choose two."

"Amazing. I've been told all this but—"

She abruptly stopped speaking, and the strange, alarmed look in her eyes caught his attention. As did the fact that what he could see of her face not covered by her mask had flushed scarlet. What was all that about?

"Told all this?" he prompted.

"Nothing. I mean, in nursing school I'd been told it. Learned about it."

She turned away, busying herself with checking Angela's vital signs. Aaron studied her another moment, then dismissed his thought that she'd suddenly acted strange. Probably imagining it.

"So that's it," he said, leaning back and gathering the dishes he'd placed the fluids in as the ultrasound technician cleaned up her things and left the room. "Do you need to check on your patient, or do you have time to wake Angela? If you can, I'll check on her and prescribe some pain meds, then have someone keep an eye on her for about an hour before she's discharged."

"Let me check on my patient, then I'll let you know one way or another, though I expect she's still far from ready to deliver." Hope stood and placed her hand on his shoulder. "I want to tell you that what you do is so impressive. So wonderful that doctors like you can give people who can't have babies the family they want. It's... You have to feel great about that."

"All doctors train to help people in different ways. I like what I do, but it probably isn't quite as important as brain surgery or treating someone's cancer." He didn't add that in addition to helping people create the baby they desperately wanted, his mission was to help prevent the kind of tragedy his own family had suffered.

"Those are important, yes. But believe me when I say that what you do is incredibly important too." To his surprise, she leaned down and pressed her lips to his forehead, and, even though she still had on her paper mask, it felt nice. Nice enough that he wanted to stand up and press his own mouth to hers to see if a paper-mask kiss with her might almost be better than a real kiss with anyone else.

He shook his head at the stupid thought. After only one night, the woman had bewitched him, and he knew at that moment he couldn't just accept her telling him more time together was out of the question without understanding why. Without pursuing her a little more to see if, maybe, she didn't really mean it after all.

"Since you're so interested in the procedure, could you find time around one p.m. today to come watch the fertilization process? It's pretty incredible to see. I think you'd be fascinated."

"I'd love that, and I'll be off work by then." Her eyes shone at him over her mask, then the glow faded. "I do have an appointment though, and I'm not sure how long it will take. But if I can be there, I will. I'll go check on my patient and be right back."

He watched her leave the room, and it was hard to imagine there could be anything sexy about her loose scrubs, her golden hair tucked into a paper hat, or the flapping paper gown concealing any curves. But he knew what that beautiful body of hers looked like underneath all that, and his heart stepped up its pace as he remembered.

He pressed his fingers to his own pulse and shook his head at himself, wondering what the heck it was about Hope Sanders that had him feeling like an adolescent with his first crush.

Whatever it was, he had no idea. And, yeah, this strange preoccupation and restlessness clearly showed that he needed to think hard about what his next job might look like. He didn't belong in Cambridge. He didn't belong anywhere.

But until he moved on, changing her mind about the two of them spending time together just became his priority. What better way to celebrate the Christmas season?

CHAPTER FOUR

HOW IN THE world had it not occurred to her what a massive and embarrassing problem this could be? As if she weren't already a bit nervous anyway, and this situation compounded the jitter of her nerves tenfold.

With her heart fluttering in her throat, Hope practically tiptoed into the offices the IVF physicians at CRMU shared. She peeked through the fingers she held up to the side of her face to see if Dr. Aaron Cartwright would be inopportunely standing there. As though her hand would somehow, magically, make her unrecognizable even if he was.

An invisibility potion was what she really needed. Or a new brain.

The only people in sight were the receptionist behind the front desk and one patient sitting in the small waiting room. She huffed out a relieved breath and, with her legs feeling a little jelly-like, stepped to the glass window. The receptionist slid it open with a smile.

"May I help you?"

Help her with that new brain thing, maybe. "I'm Hope Sanders." Would the woman think it odd that she was whispering, or just assume she had laryngitis? She glanced all around behind the receptionist, praying she didn't see a tall, brown-haired hunk of a doctor back there. "I have a noon appointment with Dr. Devor."

"Ah. Well." The woman's face lost its smile, instead turning somehow frowning and apologetic at the same time, which seemed a little odd to Hope. But then again, Hope's tentative steps, whispering and furtive looks probably seemed even more odd. "Come with me, please."

Hope followed her down a hallway until she was ushered into a small room. "Make yourself comfortable. The office manager, Sue Calloway, will be right with you."

Trying to occupy herself and forget the possibility of seeing Aaron Cartwright, and what in the world she'd say if she did, she picked up literature invitingly placed in cardboard holders on a side table. She tried to flip through it, but couldn't focus on the illustrations and information. And really didn't need to, because after all she'd seen the amazing egg-retrieval procedure on that monitor today very clearly. Calmly and oh-so-skillfully done by Aaron, his dark eyes focused and intent on the monitor. Not a single hesitation in his movements throughout the entire thing, he was obviously supremely confident in his work.

Supremely confident as a lover, as well.

Sighing, Hope closed her eyes, and images of their evening together filled her mind. The carved planes of his handsome face, his brown eyes looking at her with humor and heat. The heart-stopping beauty of his muscular physique, lying over her, pressed against her.

The sensations, too. The deep, hot, mind-blowing kisses that nearly melted her to the floor. The shivery feel of his fingers stroking her skin. The masculine scent of him in her nostrils as she kissed and licked his strong jaw, his throat, his chest. She breathed through her nose, imagining it all, sinking into thoughts of him and what they'd done together until her heart was tripping as though he really were there.

The thought had her flinging her eyelids open

and sitting bolt upright to stare at the door, then slumping back into the chair when she saw it was still closed. Lord, the memory of his scent had seemed so vivid, she'd been suddenly terrified he'd be standing right there. Asking what in the world she was doing there.

And why did it seem terrifying, anyway?

She stood and paced the small room. A one-night fling with a super-sexy man was just that. It had no impact or influence on the decision she'd made to have a baby now while she still could. She knew what she wanted and wasn't ashamed of it. Hadn't made the decision hastily. Her mother fully supported her. Which were the only things that mattered. Certainly not the briefest of relationships, so she shouldn't have even the slightest funny feeling about it.

At the same time, it was a very private thing, wasn't it? She didn't want to share it with the world yet, especially since she had no idea whether things would go as she planned or not. Despite wanting to keep it to herself for now, she feared lying wouldn't work if Aaron saw her there. It had never come easily to her and he'd probably see through it anyway. So what could be her excuse, then? *Oh, I'm doing research on IVF just because I'm interested in it.*

Not because I'm planning to get pregnant that way in just a couple of weeks.

She sighed again. At some point, he'd probably see her at work with her belly swollen. But by then, their amazing evening together would be a distant memory, wouldn't it? It was the "right now," just days after they'd made love, that must be making her feel so strange about him finding out her plans.

She tensed as the door opened, but it was a short, middle-aged woman, and not, thankfully, Aaron. Presumably the office manager she'd been told to expect.

"Hello!" The woman held out her hand. "I'm Sue Calloway. I run this place, and don't let any of the doctors tell you otherwise."

Hope liked her cheerful smile immediately. "My mother always says that women run the world and men take the credit for it."

"True. Very true." Sue nodded and chuckled, then her mirth faded and she gestured for Hope to sit down. "Part of running this place is giving patients unfortunate news. Which is that Dr.

Devor has had to leave Cambridge to tend to a family emergency and won't be back until probably next week, or possibly longer."

"Oh no!" Hope stared at her, heart sinking. Next week? What a disappointing delay!

But the peculiar feeling that instantly rolled around in her gut at the news had her wondering about that thought. Because the feeling seemed just as much relief as dismay, and how could that be? Yes, she was a little scared. But from the time she was a teen, she'd pictured two things in her life. Becoming a certified midwife, and holding her own baby in her arms.

Anger joined the other confusing emotions churning in her chest. Why had she listened to her parents' insistence that she couldn't do both at the same time, just because they hadn't been able to? Just because they'd gotten married too young because her mum was pregnant, and didn't even like each other much?

Their battles eventually became a cold, distant silence between the two of them, and between her and her dad, too. Doubtless all that had scarred her in some way. She knew it must be part of the reason why she'd never been able to commit to a man. Never truly loved a man.

Never truly loved George, and hoped and prayed that he was wrong. That there wasn't something utterly lacking inside her heart that would make it impossible to love anyone, including this baby she so wanted.

Her throat closed as fear clutched at her again, but she fiercely shook it off. She could love her child. She knew she could.

"You have several options, though," Sue said.

"Options?"

"Obviously, you can simply wait until Dr. Devor returns, and we'll put you at the top of his schedule then. Or you can see another of our IVF consultants to discuss the treatment options and get the necessary tests done. If you decide to go on with it, you could already be getting started on the course of hormones to stimulate your ovaries before Dr. Devor even returns."

About the only thing Hope heard the woman say was "you can see another of our IVF consultants," which sent a cold shiver down her spine, and not the good kind Aaron had sent through her whole body the other night. Imagining just running into him here was bad enough, but having him as her consultant? After they'd slept together?

Not only disturbing, but also highly unethical. What could she say to Sue, though? *Oh, well, another doctor would be fine, except not sexy Dr. Cartwright because he's already seen me completely and intimately naked.*

Sue was regarding her a bit oddly, and she wondered what she looked like, other than very, very flushed at the embarrassing thought. She cleared her throat. "Thank you for giving me some options. Since it sounds like Dr. Devor will likely return fairly soon, I think I'll just wait until then."

"Fine. I'll call you to schedule another appointment when he's back."

"That sounds perfect. Thank you."

They both stood and Sue opened the door, gesturing for her to lead the way. Hope took a few tentative steps down a short hall and into the waiting room, her nerves jangling all over again as she furtively glanced around, then practically ran out of the door, not caring if Sue thought she was a nutcase or not.

She kept going until she was a good distance

from the office before she finally slowed down, annoyed with herself that she was being such a Nervous Nellie, but unable to stop feeling that way. She pressed her hands to her hot cheeks, not paying much attention to where she was walking, until she realized she was outside the swinging doors to the hospital wing where Aaron would be fertilizing Mrs. Walters's eggs at 1:00 p.m. The ICSI procedure.

It wasn't the procedure she would be using, since traditional IVF was an easier method if the ICSI procedure wasn't necessary for success. But she'd been fascinated to see the egg retrieval today, and knew getting to see firsthand this fairly new procedure would be too. Fascinating because she was a nurse and a midwife, and because she'd be having her own IVF procedure soon.

She stared at the door, feeling indecisive and uncomfortable all over again, which was completely unlike her. Aaron had suggested she join him there for educational reasons, right? It had nothing to do with the undeniable chemistry between them that zapped in the air every time their eyes met.

Right. She shook her head and forced herself to move on down the hall and out of the door. The last thing she should do was encourage the man to think she was interested in him. She had big plans, wonderful plans, and shoving aside and trying to forget about her ridiculous attraction to Aaron Cartwright was the only sensible choice.

Aaron grabbed his briefcase of patient files to study later and took a few steps down the office hallway, poking his head into Sue's office. "My last patient canceled, so I'm heading home."

"Early for you. Hot date tonight?"

He had to chuckle at Sue's exaggerated eyebrow waggling as she asked. "Why do you want to know? Jealous?"

"I live for gossip. You know that."

"Well, I'm sorry to disappoint you, but I'm just going to take advantage of what's left of the daylight to go for a run, then do some paperwork. Excitement is my middle name."

"Hmm. Either you're not telling me the truth, or you've decided you don't want to break any more hearts right now and ruin a girl's holiday."

The truth? Truth was, the only woman he was

interested in at the moment had clearly meant it when she'd said one night was all she could offer. He'd been disappointed when she hadn't shown up to see the ICSI procedure she'd seemed so interested in, and while it was possible she'd just gotten stuck at whatever her appointment was, he had a feeling it was more that she'd decided to keep her distance.

Then the past few days, when he'd found reasons to stop into the labor and delivery ward and seen Hope at a distance, she'd given him a quick smile and wave of her fingers before practically tearing off in the other direction.

Which was a very clear message—*keep your distance, buddy.* A message that should have left him shrugging his shoulders and moving on. Problem was, he didn't want to move on right then. He wanted to spend more time enjoying her lively mind and her beautiful body. He just had to figure out a way to charm her into it.

If he ever had a chance to be near her and spend time with her again, that was. Which was looking less promising by the day.

"I don't know where you got this idea that I'm

a heartbreaker," he said. "The women I date don't expect anything long-term."

"Maybe don't expect it, but definitely want it. And why you're so determined to stay footloose and fancy-free, I don't know."

Didn't take a rocket scientist, or a shrink, to figure it out. Abandonment in childhood created adults who didn't want to risk that happening again. Moving from place to place and not getting too close to anyone or anything was the solution. Pathetic? Probably, but he'd been just fine living his life that way. "Why you're so determined to see me tied down, I don't know either. Probably so I can be as miserable as Paul is."

She tossed a wadded-up ball of paper at his head and he laughed that he'd gotten the reaction he'd wanted, and a change of subject. "See you tomorrow."

"After that insult, you'll be lucky if I'm here."

"You'll be here. Not being able to bug me every day would drive you crazy." Chuckling at the second ball of paper launched at his head and the faux outrage on her face, he ducked out of the office, only to practically knock down the receptionist.

"Sorry, Liz!" He grabbed her plump shoulders to steady her. "Sue's in a bad mood, trying to hurt me, and I wasn't looking where I was going."

"Well, this will cheer her up, but probably not you," Liz said, grinning broadly as she held up a newspaper. "She said there would be a photo of you with a woman at the gala, and she'll be happy to be right."

He sighed and put his briefcase by his feet to reach for the paper. Hopefully, the article concentrated mostly on the adoption foundation, and not on him. For whatever reason though, after the past few galas, the reporters had seemed to love to include tidbits about his background and his single status along with the important information. He didn't care much for it, but could put up with undesirable attention if it helped get the foundation the attention he worked for.

"Let me see," Sue said, practically chortling as she came to stand next to him.

"I have it folded to the photo. Page seven, on the other side." Liz tapped the paper with her finger. "He's dancing with a gorgeous blonde, and the picture practically looks like an advertisement for

Valentine's Day, the way they're making eyes at one another."

The only woman he'd danced with had been Hope, and gorgeous blonde was just a small part of the way he'd describe her. He frowned and turned the paper over. Sure enough, amid other photos of various attendees, there they were, dancing so closely their bodies were touching, and looking into one another's eyes as if there weren't another soul in the room.

Well, damn. Part of him felt a little embarrassed at what the photo revealed. But staring at the picture reminded him how stunning she'd looked that night. Her sweet smile. Her intelligent, amused eyes. The beautiful curve of her lips.

The memory of it all hit him almost as though she were in his arms again. The feel of the smooth skin of her back against his palm, the way her curves fit his body as they danced, the scent of her in his nose and the mesmerizing blue of her eyes as they met his.

His memories moved on to the incredible bliss they'd shared later that night in glorious Technicolor, and his damned mindless body actually started to physically react. He folded the paper with a snap. "I'll read it later. Make a note, Sue, to get the newspaper reporter and photographer to the Christmas adoption party, so they can get more important photos of adoptable kids meeting potential parents."

"I already have, and you know it. It's not my fault they took this kind of pic, which I know you hate." She tugged at the paper. "Might as well let me see it, because I get it at home anyway."

"You live for gossip, all right. Especially when it involves me." He grimaced at her and handed it over. If he didn't, it would make it seem suspiciously an even bigger deal. He braced himself, knowing Sue would tease him about the way he and Hope were looking all starstruck at one another. How had she managed to make him forget everything in the room but her? "Fine. But I don't want to hear anything more about it."

"Oh, you two *are* making goo-goo eyes at one another! She—"

To his surprise, Sue stopped in mid-sentence, and the mirth in her face disappeared as she stared at the photo, then slowly moved her gaze up to Aaron. Her expression was so oddly, well, *stunned* was the word that came to mind, it was downright strange. "What? What's with the weird face? You're looking at me like it's a picture of me dancing with the queen. Or the devil."

"No. I just—she's a midwife here at CRMU, right?"

"Right. She's one of several that came to share a few adoption stories with donors, which I appreciated. Then we danced, and that photo is ridiculous, because we weren't making goo-goo eyes at each other at all. So don't act like there's some big meaning behind it." He wasn't about to share anything else, or admit that the picture captured exactly how he'd been feeling at that moment.

Captivated and aroused.

"I won't. Of course it's just a meaningless picture of a brief moment. You don't have any real interest in her, do you?"

She sounded almost hopeful, which was also very strange, since she was always nagging him about finding the right woman and settling down, despite him always responding that he had zero interest in that. "No. We were just dancing." And that was a lie, but his interest in Hope wasn't anyone's business.

Sue put on a smile that seemed oddly forced

as she folded the newspaper and gave it back to Liz. Which was one more bizarre thing, since in the past when things like this had happened she'd loved parading it around the office to show everyone. What in the world was making her act so strange?

Not that he was unhappy about closing the newspaper and the subject. "I'm heading out. See you in the morning."

The photo of him and Hope swam in his mind, and damned if part of him wanted to swing through Labor and Delivery again just to look at her in person. Maybe see if she'd be off work soon.

Then reminded himself about her not wanting any more contact between them. Since when had he wanted to be an annoyance to a woman? If she wasn't interested, there were others who were. And yeah, maybe this strange preoccupation with her really was a sign he'd been in Cambridge too long.

He strode down the hall toward the parking garage and glanced at the weather report on his phone, glad to see it was warm enough outside that he could take his run wearing a single layer of clothes. Running hard and building up a sweat would both relax his tight muscles after doing procedures all day, and get his one-track mind off Hope Sanders.

"Help! I have an emergency!" a woman's voice shouted. "I need a delivery doctor right away! Can anyone help?"

CHAPTER FIVE

AARON TURNED TOWARD the loud, anxious voice, astonished to see Hope Sanders literally running down the hall full steam, pushing a patient on a cart and craning her neck to look in various open doors as she shouted. A nurse followed just as fast, and he pivoted in their direction, then strode beside her as she kept up her fast pace.

"What's wrong?" He glanced at the moaning woman on the cart. "What do you need?"

"I have a shoulder dystocia. Can't move the baby into position. The doctors on call are busy with at-risk births and there's no time to lose. I'm getting her to the OR now."

"Why do you think it's shoulder dystocia?" he asked, tossing his briefcase on a nurse's desk as they hurried by.

"The head crowned, then turtled back against the perineum and the baby's cheeks bulged out," she continued in a tight, breathless voice as she swung the cart through the OR doors with re-markable precision, considering she'd barely slowed down.

Damn. Definitely dystocia, which had to be dealt with immediately, or the baby could be either seriously injured or die. And Aaron hadn't dealt with one since his obstetrics training in the United States, and then only a few times.

"I thought the dad was going to faint, so he's been taken to the waiting room," Hope said.

"All right." He quickly scrubbed, then snapped on gloves as Hope and the nurse got the patient set up in the room. The moaning, obviously terrified mother stared at him as he stood in front of her, Hope beside him.

"Is it okay? Oh, my God," she cried, her moan morphing into a wail.

"Let's see what's going on," Aaron said. Keeping his voice calm and soothing was an effort when he saw what he and Hope were dealing with here. Every muscle tensed and he took a deep breath, working to keep his calm and remember his training. "How long do you think it's been since the baby's head crowned?"

"Probably only a minute. I knew I had to get

help immediately." Hope pressed the microphone around her neck. "I'll get Neonatal on the line now."

"Good. Anesthesia, too, in case we have to C-section. Nurse, I need you to keep track of the time, and call out every thirty seconds that pass. Mom, what's happening here is that the baby's shoulder is stuck on your pelvis. I'm going to try to release it, okay?"

Her answer was another wail as he used the various maneuvers that sometimes worked in a situation like this. "Sorry. Hang in there. Big baby we've got here."

Hope anticipated every action as they worked together to release the baby's shoulder, but it was still jammed tight like a branch in a river rock.

"Thirty seconds," the nurse said.

Sweat pricked Aaron's skin as Hope's intense eyes met his, and he knew she was thinking exactly what he was. That if they couldn't get the baby out within moments, the chances of it being healthy and undamaged were damned unlikely.

"Is anesthesia on the way? No choice but to do the Zavanelli maneuver. Get her prepped for C-section. Make it a flash and dash to get the

Betadine on in a hurry. Not low transverse, classical. You know time is critical. Then get scrubbed to assist."

She gave him a quick nod. "Got it."

Aaron sucked in another calming breath as he worked to maneuver the baby back to a position they could deliver it with a C-section. Hope quickly swabbed the woman's belly with antiseptic. Anesthesia ran in, and Aaron sent up a silent prayer of thanks that the troops had arrived. Except they were far from out of the woods.

"Need general anesthesia, and some Versed too. Hang in there for us, Mom."

"Oh, God," the mother said again, gasping, her eyes already closing, her words slurred. "My baby. Is it going…to be…all right?"

"Doing the best we can." He didn't know the answer to her question, but he damned well was going to get the baby out as fast as possible to increase the odds of it surviving. Aaron tensely watched the anesthesia team get the patient intubated. "Is she ready?"

"She's out. Good to go."

"I'm ready, too, Doctor," Hope said next to him.

"Good. Nurse, hand me the knife. Hope, I'm going to need you to help me from below."

"I'm getting baby moved up a little more," Hope said, her eyes fierce with concentration. "It's... it's fully back in her uterus now."

"Good. I'm going to get started. Neonatal here yet?"

"Not yet," Hope answered, her voice tense and worried.

"I need you to assist. Get ready to resuscitate baby and run it to the special care baby unit if Neonatal's not here in time."

"I'm ready."

Aaron began the section and got the baby exposed as quickly as possible. He reached to lift the baby boy out, gritting his teeth at the infant's dangerously deep purple color. If they didn't get him breathing in short order, he either wouldn't make it, or there'd be damage to his brain.

He quickly wiped the baby's face, but knew Hope and the nurse would do a better job with cleaning the baby and getting it breathing than he would remember how to do.

As he passed the infant to Hope his eyes briefly met hers. Intense blue eyes that reflected back the same concern he had about the baby's chances before she quickly focused with deep concentration on the infant.

"Is the Ambu bag ready?" Hope asked the nurse without looking up as she swiftly and efficiently suctioned the baby's mouth and nose.

"Right here."

Hope reached for it, placing the oxygen mask over the child's nose and mouth as she instructed the nurse to rub the baby with a towel to dry and warm him. Just as Aaron was about to turn to the mother the rest of the cavalry ran into the room. He huffed out a giant breath of relief. Had to be the neonatal team, ready to assist Hope and take over. Then it was time to pray like hell for the little guy.

He watched for a second to see Hope pass the baby to the neonatal team. They wasted no time getting the baby resuscitated and stabilized as they checked his heart rate. Aaron sent up a silent prayer of thanks that the infant's color already seemed a little better.

He refocused on the still-unconscious mother, who'd been through quite an ordeal, and got started repairing her incision. He could hear Hope briefing the neonatal team. Calm, composed information and questions, which was impressive, since he knew she had to be feeling the same adrenaline rush and stress he did.

"Baby's in good hands, Dr. Cartwright," Hope said from across the room. "I'll scrub again, then I'll help you close."

"Good." He wasn't about to say, *I can use all the help I can get* and let everyone in the room know he was a little rusty at surgery, but had a feeling Hope already knew that.

Hope stood next to him, her arm pressing against his as they worked together. He glanced down at her and their eyes met again. This time, hers were smiling. "Impressive work, Dr. Cartwright. No one would ever guess you didn't deliver babies every day, especially tough ones like this."

"Doubt that's true, but thanks. And you were pretty impressive yourself, diagnosing the problem instantly, getting her down to the OR and getting big baby pushed back up in time for me to get him out fast. We made a pretty good team, I think."

"Yeah. We did." Their eyes met again, held,

and this time there was an odd, serious note in her eyes along with that smile and a clear admiration that made him feel pretty damned happy he'd been in the right place at the right time.

"Did Neonatal get cord blood to check baby's gases?"

"Yes. They sent it to the lab stat, so we should know his PH soon. I'm praying he's okay."

So was Aaron. He'd almost forgotten how amazing it was to help bring a baby into the world and felt an attachment to the little guy. "How's his anterior shoulder and arm?"

"Not moving it quite as well as he should, but the pediatrician said she thinks it's going to be fine."

"Good."

They finished the repair in silence, Hope again working efficiently, anticipating everything he needed before he had to ask. "Okay." He sat back and snapped off his gloves. "We can slow down her meds now and get Mom waking up," he said to the anesthesiologist. "Nurse, can you take care of Mom and get her to Recovery while Hope and I go talk to the family?"

"Yes, Doctor."

The two of them walked together toward the waiting room, and the same sense of connection he'd felt with Hope from the moment they'd first spent time together was there, but magnified times ten. He knew it was probably because they'd gone through such an intense procedure together with a baby's life on the line, but it was a sensation he wasn't familiar with. Didn't know what to do with, either.

"Let's see if we can get the PH test results before we talk to family. If he's healthy we can pass that good news on, but if we're not sure yet it would make sense to gently prepare them for the possibility that he'd gone without oxygen a little too long and will have to be evaluated."

"I agree." She talked into the little microphone around her neck, then looked up at him, her blue eyes lit with joy. "PH was seven point four! Clearly no brain damage. He's going to be just fine."

"Thank God." The relief that swept through him was surprisingly intense. Despite the stress of it all, he realized he was glad he'd had this experience today. Helping people conceive, being there for them for both success and failure, was what he did every day. Bringing that baby into the world was an entirely different kind of important. A reminder, really, that when he helped a couple get pregnant the end result was an incredible miracle. "You did it, Hope. You got him to the OR, then stabilized and bagged in the nick of time."

"No, we did it. And Mum is all right, too, thanks to you." Her elated and admiring gaze met his, and just as his chest began to fill with the same emotion she surprised him by practically launching herself at him, flinging her arms around his neck. A laugh bubbled from her lips as his arms wrapped around her, too. As if they belonged there. "Thank God you were in the hall when I came looking for help. You were amazing."

"Like we said before, it was a team effort, Hope." He couldn't stop his hand from gently smoothing back strands of hair on her forehead that had escaped her ponytail. "You were more than amazing, and have a lot to be proud of today."

"We do." To his shock and utter pleasure, she gave him a big, smacking kiss on the lips, and he had to force himself to not go back for one less celebratory and a lot more sensual.

"I have to tell you though, for a minute there I was really worried," she said. "When you couldn't get him loose, even after you tried to turn him several different ways, and his color was so ghastly, I really thought it might be too late."

"For the record, I was a little worried, too." He pressed his mouth to her ear. "Don't tell anybody, but I've never delivered a shoulder dystocia by myself before."

"What? That makes it even more amazing!" Her eyes widened. "I guess I should have realized. You help people make babies, you don't deliver them. When was the last time you did?"

"Obviously, during my obstetrics training I delivered a lot of babies, but not since then. And dystocia is pretty rare, as you know, though I hear it's getting more common with bigger babies being born."

"He was a big one, wasn't he? I hope I don't have to go through that again any time soon." Unfortunately, she seemed to realize she was clinging to his neck and drew back. While Aaron liked her just where she was, her body pressed all warm and soft against his, he figured the hospital hallway didn't provide the kind of privacy he found himself wishing for at that moment.

A man leaped up the second they stepped into the waiting room, and Hope approached him with a smile. "First, Mum and baby are doing fine, Mr. Smith. And second, it's a boy! Congratulations."

"Oh, thank God. Thank you. Thank you so much."

The man's voice was choked, and his eyes puddled up as he pumped Hope's hand. Aaron felt relieved all over again that they were able to give him good news, when it had been too damned close to being the opposite.

"This is Dr. Cartwright, who delivered your son. I'll let him explain what had to happen."

"Hope probably told you the baby's shoulder was lodged into your wife's pubic bone. We did what we could to get him loose, but in the end had to do a Cesarean section. Being stuck in the birth canal like that is traumatizing to a baby, and we had to deliver him fast. But as Hope told you, your wife is fine and your son is fine. Quite a bruiser, too—I predict he'll be a damn good rugby player someday."

The man laughed and swiped at his eyes. "Can I see them?"

"Baby is in the SCBU, on the second floor," Hope said. "I'll meet you there in a few minutes, then take you, and baby, too, if I get the green light, to see your wife."

The man again profusely thanked them and left, leaving Aaron to enjoy the smiling blue of Hope's eyes for another minute. And he realized that, despite telling himself he needed to be, he wasn't ready to accept her insistence that one evening together was all they could have.

Why he wanted to convince a woman to be with him if she didn't want to be, he didn't know, but he wasn't going to waste time wondering. And with any luck, today's events just might have provided him with a damned good bargaining tool.

"I think a celebration is in order, don't you?" he asked, looking down into Hope's glowing eyes. "How about we do that punting you're dying to learn how to do, then have a drink in honor of Mom and big bruiser? I checked the weather just a little while ago, and it really is balmy right now. Honest."

"I...I..."

He hated to see her joyous smile fade, her face turn away from him slightly to look over his shoulder at the wall. He grasped her chin in his fingers to bring her gaze back to him, and the troubled expression on her face made it difficult to keep his tone light. "Are you saying 'Aye-aye, Captain,' in anticipation of our boating expedition? What time are you off?"

"I'm working late, actually. Sorry."

Well, damned if her voice and expression weren't both equally stiff now. The part of him that knew he should go right back to what he'd decided earlier, which was to forget about her and whatever reason she had for not wanting to spend time with him, was overwhelmed by the chemistry between them. An attraction that sizzled every bit as much as it had the other night whether she liked it or not.

He dropped his hand from her chin and glanced around. The few people nearby were doing their jobs, and didn't seem particularly interested in watching the two of them. "Is that true, or an excuse because you don't want to go out with me?"

"Okay." Her gaze met his squarely. "I'm not

working late. It's just that, like I said before, we can't date."

Those blue eyes might be trying to look decisive and firm, but he was pretty sure the little pucker between her brows showed confusion. And he knew damned well the heat sparking between them didn't go just one way. Did it?

"That you would fib about that gouges right into my heart, you know."

"Uh-huh. As though I could hurt Dr. Aaron Cartwright's feelings." The eye roll she gave didn't completely conceal the flicker of worry on her face that maybe she actually had, and he had to smile at how sweet she was.

"You might be surprised." He didn't share his feelings easily, but he sure as hell had them. Especially around her. At the moment, those feelings were pushing him to coerce her into saying "yes" to a little more time together, good idea or not. "All I'm suggesting is a little celebration of our success, and for one of Cambridge's lifelong citizens to learn punting so she doesn't embarrass her hometown. But if you won't join me, I'll just go home and celebrate with a beer all by my lonesome, even though I did come to your rescue."

"Not my rescue, the mum and baby's rescue." She folded her arms across her chest, but the amusement in her eyes that suddenly replaced the worry had him hopeful that she just might cave and forget whatever concerns she had. "Why I'm letting you twist my arm this way, I don't know," she said, shaking her head. "After I take Mr. Smith to see his wife and possibly bring baby to her as well, I'll get cleaned up. I'll meet you at the dock by that pub we went by the…the other night."

Her face flushed as soon as she finished the sentence. The last thing he wanted was for memories of that night to make her change her mind, though how that could happen, he couldn't imagine. Lord knew those memories were part of what made him determined to be with her again. "Listen, I rode my bike to work, but how about I ride it home now to get my car and pick you up here in, say, an hour instead of meeting you there?"

"You rode your bike?" Those pretty pink lips of hers parted in surprise. "I rode my bike, too, since it was such a nice day."

"See there? It was meant to be." And it was. He'd felt that way the minute he'd met her, and this was more proof they were destined to spend some time together for a while. "We can enjoy the warm, late afternoon sun by riding along the river, have our punting lesson, then eat pub food. I'll meet you at the north bike racks in an hour."

He almost turned to walk away, not wanting to give her the chance to say no, but knew that would be rude. So he waited, his chest feeling a little tighter with each long beat that passed, wondering why her answer mattered so much. Why he felt nearly weak with relief when she finally nodded. "All right. An hour."

"Good." He headed back toward the nurses' station where he'd left his briefcase, resisting the urge to look back at her. Wishing she'd been smiling when she'd answered, instead of so serious-looking, but he'd take what he could get.

With any luck, Hope really did want to be with him this evening and didn't just feel obligated after he'd been so pushy about it. That kind of question had never entered his mind before on past dates, and he didn't like it that he had to wonder about it now. But however their evening together went, for better or for worse, it was more than worth finding the answer.

CHAPTER SIX

THE EVENING SUN glowed low on the horizon, casting fingers of brilliant gold through the barren trees and across the landscape, turning the still green grass to a cheerful chartreuse. Hope breathed in the clear air, her chest somehow light and energized at the same time her tummy tightened with misgiving, wondering what in the world she was doing.

She dared to glance at the man riding beside her, the sun gleaming on his chestnut hair and movie-star-handsome face. Sunglasses covered his eyes, and he wore a fairly tight-fitting, long-sleeved athletic shirt that molded itself to the contours of his muscular arms and torso, and *whoo, boy*, were those contours very, very sexy.

He must have felt her looking at him, as he turned to her and smiled. The curve of his lips was sexy, too, and why was she out here tempting herself with this *über*-attractive man when any kind of relationship was out of the question?

The rapid beat of her heart gave her the unwelcome answer, and it wasn't because she was riding the bicycle. The pace they kept was pretty modest, and as she focused her attention on the river path she couldn't deny the truth.

She was out here with him because she wanted to be.

Which made her one confused woman. Then again, he wasn't a man who was looking for anything long-term, so her inadequacy in that arena didn't matter, right? She didn't have to understand love and relationships to get all hot and bothered just by looking at him. To want to sink into his kisses and enjoy the feel of his arms around her holding her close one more time.

She stole another glance at him, and darn it if he wasn't still smiling at her, looking as though he was thoroughly enjoying this ride with her. And if he was, that made it okay, didn't it? Enjoy a little harmless fun together just once more, with no expectations for anything more, like lots of singles did all the time.

The thought reassured and relaxed her, and she

inwardly laughed at herself for making all of this a bigger thing than it was.

"There's a bike rack down here. Follow me," Aaron said, speeding up to take the lead.

They rode single file down a small incline to a rack filled with bicycles. Aaron slowed to a stop and shoved his front wheel into a slot before coming to grasp the handlebars of hers as she balanced on it. The path was shadowed here, and he slipped off his sunglasses, tucking them into the neck of his shirt before he reached for the clip of her helmet.

"Instead of messing with my helmet, maybe you should try wearing one of your own," she said, brushing aside his fingers to undo the clip herself, at the same time hoping to also brush aside the tingles that simple touch had sent down her throat. "I would think every doctor was well acquainted with the dangers of a head injury."

He smiled, and as she stared at the curve of his lips she nearly forgot to remove her helmet after she'd unclipped it. Her hair tangled a little inside it as she pulled it off, and she was trying to shake it loose when his fingers set it free, gently combing through it.

"If I'm racing, or skiing fast, I wear one. But meandering down a river trail? I'd rather feel the wind on my head."

"You can fall and hit your head on cement just straddling a bike," she said, intentionally sounding like a scolding schoolmarm in the hopes that he wouldn't notice how his touch made her heart go into a near arrhythmia. Trying not to think about how hunky he looked in his athletic clothes with his thick hair all tousled from said wind. With a five o'clock shadow darkening his sculpted jaw.

She asked herself why she'd wanted to come out with him again. The clear, gorgeous answer was right in front of her, enough to tempt any woman with a beating heart. Which hers was currently doing in double time.

Those chocolatey brown eyes of his crinkled at the corners as his gaze captured hers. "Well, all of life's a risk, isn't it?"

Yes, it sure was. She had a very big feeling that being here with him tonight posed some kind of serious risk, but what exactly that risk was she didn't know. Consequences, maybe, too?

She definitely hoped not. But it was her last

chance for a little pre-baby, pre-changed-life fun, right? Before she devoted herself to loving her baby, proving she was as capable of that as anyone who'd always wanted a child. Proving George wrong.

Gulping in some courage, Hope got off her bike. Surely she'd look back on this evening and mock herself about silly thoughts of risks and consequences from a simple night out with a man.

Aaron's big hand engulfed hers as they walked to the punts. "Are you ready for your first lesson?"

"Not sure. Will I embarrass myself?"

"The only possible way you could embarrass yourself is if you get so frustrated you throw the pole overboard. Which I've seen happen. If you just plan to have fun learning, you'll be fine."

She had to laugh. "I admit I like to be good at whatever I do, but I think I'm mature enough to know that everything takes practice. So I'll go for the fun, and shove the competitive Hope under the punt."

"I admit I'd enjoy seeing the competitive Hope some time. Very intriguing to wonder what she would be like," he said with a teasing look.

"She can be scary. Especially in sports. In school once, I was so intent on getting the net-ball in the hoop I cracked heads with another girl and nearly knocked both of us out."

"Now I understand your nagging about the bike helmet," he said, laughing. "The good news is you're not likely to crack your head open punting even if you fall out, so you can forgo the helmet. Though you do look very cute in it."

He'd leaned close as he spoke, his voice a sexy deep rumble in her ear that gave her bad thoughts. Thoughts of ditching this punting lesson to sug-gest something a lot more fun.

She yanked her thoughts back to what they'd been talking about before. If she could remem-ber what it was. Oh, yes. Helmets and punting.

"Helmets are not cute, but they are practical," she said, conjuring the schoolmarm voice again in the hopes that he didn't notice her slight breath-lessness.

"And you're a very practical woman. Some-times." That teasing glint was back in his eyes, and she tried to ignore its appeal. "I assume you swim, but if you go overboard I promise I'll come rescue you."

"I swim very well, thank you. And I'm quite certain I won't go overboard."

"Don't be so certain. Especially if you, as a Cambridge native, insist on punting Cambridge style."

"Cambridge style?"

They'd reached the dock and Aaron answered as he arranged to rent the boat. "Standing on the till—the flat part at the stern. In Oxford, punters stand inside the boat and punt with the till forward. Both groups think their way is the right way, and are sure anyone who does it different is all wrong."

"And how does an American know all this when I've never heard it?"

He flashed her that quick grin again, more dazzling than the evening sun. "Because I've punted plenty of times with both groups in both places. Pretty amusing to sit back and hear them argue about it, because in Colorado we use both techniques, depending on how fast the water is. And I also know this because I'm an expert at many, many things."

Which she already knew. "There's that ego thing again," she said lightly, hoping he didn't know that memories of his expertise instantly came to mind in glorious detail.

He grinned and reached for her hand again as she stepped into the punt, then followed her as the boat gently rocked. "We'll do it Cambridge style, since we don't want fingers pointing at us, do we? How about I go first so you can watch, then you can take over?"

"Sounds like a good plan." She'd watched plenty of punting in her life without paying much attention to the technique. But watching his muscular physique in that tight shirt of his as he did? Thinking about his various techniques at everything from doctoring to lovemaking? Not something she was going to argue with or complain about.

She settled onto the bench seat, more than happy to be facing him because, as she'd suspected, the moment he pushed the pole into the water his biceps bulged and his pectorals flexed and she wondered if she could convince him to forget the teaching part of it all so she could just keep admiring him.

The boat slid smoothly across the water, away from the other boats cruising the river. Aaron's gaze moved from the river to her and back, and she was struck all over again at how beautiful he truly was, with his chiseled features relaxed, his hair all messy, a smile of pure pleasure on his face. Yes, this man was very different from the busy, serious doctor she'd noticed from afar at the hospital.

This man was testosterone on a stick, and pure fun to boot.

"I don't know, you haven't convinced me it's hard. Slide the pole in and push, then do it again. Easy." The second the words came out of her mouth she sat up straight, blushing from head to toe. Hoping against hope that he hadn't really been listening.

How ridiculous and…and horrifying that her comment had instantly made her think of sex. Was it because she'd said it to Aaron? She glanced away at the water so he couldn't see her eyes. And prayed he wasn't a mind reader.

"Sometimes easy, sometimes…hard."

His eyes gleamed wickedly at her, and she felt beyond thankful for the cool air against her hot cheeks. Lord, she had to be more careful when she talked, and, if at all possible, careful with her thoughts, too. Clearly a challenge in the company of Aaron Cartwright.

"Something a Cambridge native will be interested to know?" he said as he smoothly sent the boat downstream. "Most of the punts we used in Denver were fiberglass and made right here in your fair city."

"Really? I find that hard to believe. I would think all kinds of American boat companies would make them."

"There's not really a lot of punting in the States, to be honest. It's more of a niche thing for boaters. Plus those of us who do punt bow to England's long tradition and expertise."

They glided on in a silence that was peaceful and quiet and yet still that zing she inexplicably couldn't help but feel around him seemed to be right there in the boat, swirling in the air around them as their eyes met. As they smiled at one another, the pleasure of it seeped into every cell in her body, making her feel relaxed and energized at the same time. If she'd ever felt this way around George, maybe she would have agreed to marry him.

She sat bolt upright, shocked at the thought.

She hadn't been able to marry George, couldn't love him, because there was something missing inside her. She knew that, knew the distance and near dislike between her parents, the distance between her and her dad, too, had frozen that ability somehow. Made it impossible for her to know how to love someone.

George had been right about that. But not about loving the baby she'd wanted for so long. That he was wrong about. Had to be.

The long, peaceful glide of the punt down the river eased the tightness that had squeezed her chest. Helped release the unwelcome worries that surely happened to anyone making a big life decision. By the time Aaron nosed the boat to a part of the river where there wasn't a soul in sight, she felt relaxed again. Back to normal and able to enjoy the beautiful evening. He pulled the pole close to the side of the little boat, somehow bringing it to a standstill.

"A nice, empty place to practice. Come on. Your turn."

She didn't particularly want a turn, but he held out his hand and she stood, placing hers in his as the boat rocked a little. He drew her close and just as she thought he might kiss her, her heart thumping hard as she tried to decide what she wanted to do if he did, he turned her around to face the bow. One strong arm came around her stomach, and his pelvis bumped into her lower back, which did nothing to bring her heart rate back to normal.

"Spread your legs a bit for balance. Take the pole in both hands. I was lucky to get the spruce wood one, even though the rental places always have a lot more that are aluminum. The wood ones are warmer to hold, and more responsive, too."

Maybe she was made of wood. Since she was feeling very warm and responsive to the closeness of his body, the rumble of his voice, the brush of his breath against her cheek. *Concentrate*, she scolded herself.

"Okay." She grasped the pole and knew her voice was about as shallow as the river, but what could she do?

"So thrust the pole downward, close to the side of the punt. Let it drop to the bottom, then use both hands to bring it up to your chest, which will propel the boat forward in a nice, long stroke. Like this."

He kept his arm around her waist, and one hand below hers on the pole. Together they drew it in, her hands ending up against her breasts and his, warm and firm, against her abdomen. So intensely aware of every one of those tingly sensations, she hardly noticed the punt glide forward.

"After the stroke, just relax and let the pole float up, then we'll do it again."

Okay, enough. She relaxed her hold on the pole and sucked in a calming breath at the same time a laugh bubbled in her throat. She fisted her free hand on her hip and turned her head to look up at his face, so intimately close to hers. "Now I know why you wanted to teach me this. Is this sport always full of sexual innuendo, or just when you're the instructor?"

"What do you mean?" His fingers opened on the pole as he held it out, his expression the picture of innocence. At the same time the brown eyes crinkling at the corners held a superheated gleam. "If you were taking lessons at a club, those would be the official instructions."

"Maybe so. But you have to admit that talking

about spreading legs, warm and responsive poles, and stroking then relaxing is about as sexual a conversation as a person can have."

"Maybe it's your interpretation of it, and not the conversation itself." His head dipped to touch his mouth to her cheek, slipping it over to her ear and making her shiver. "Could it be that, unconsciously, you want it to be sexual? And maybe I'm subconsciously wanting the same thing."

She had a feeling there was no maybe about it for either of them. Hope let her head tip back against his collarbone and closed her eyes, giving herself up to the pleasure of his warm mouth on her skin. Trailing along her jaw in a breathlessly slow journey to eventually rest against the corner of her mouth.

She turned, his arm sliding along her belly around to her back, and their eyes met for a long, hungry moment before he kissed her. Her eyes slid closed as she sank into the intoxicating taste of Aaron. She let go of the pole completely, wanting to wrap her arms around his neck and pull him even closer, wanting to feel the solid strength of him pressed tightly against her body.

Perfection. Wasn't it? Warm and heady perfection. Just as she'd thought when they'd swayed together on that dance floor, and as they'd made love, their bodies seemed to be designed to fit together.

The arm that had been wrapped around her so tightly loosened, then dropped away for a split second until she could feel the heat from his palm through her shirt as it tracked to her side. Across her belly and up to cup her breast through her clothes. It felt so good, a little inarticulate sound formed in the middle of their kiss, and he pulled back an inch. The eyes staring into hers were half-mast and rich as the darkest Belgian chocolate. "You're so damn soft, so beautiful. I love to touch you. Love the feel of you."

His touch, his words, his mouth devouring hers again sent flames licking across her skin. When he lifted his hand from her breast, she opened her mouth to protest, but she thought, *Why?* His fingers slipped under her shirt to gently caress her quivering stomach then slide inside her bra to thumb her nipple.

This time, the sound she made was more like a moan. Which quickly changed to a yelp as the boat jerked with a solid thud, jolting loose the lovely warm palm cupping her breast and making her take a stumbling side step. The pole in Aaron's hand jabbed hard into her spine before clattering to the side of the boat and diving straight into the water.

"Well, hell! Sit down for a sec."

Aaron grasped her shoulders to steady her, then jumped into action. Her legs shaky, she lowered herself to the seat and watched Aaron kneel and try in vain to reach the pole, finally sticking both arms all the way into the water, sweeping them as if he were doing the breaststroke.

A different version of which he'd just been doing to her, the enjoyment of which had left the punt without a captain.

Hope had to giggle at the whole situation with the punt still knocking against the bank and the pole still escaping. "Are you going to have to jump in to get it?"

"I hope not." He kept paddling, slowly moving the punt away from the bank and toward the middle of the river in chase. "You said you're a good swimmer. Feel like practicing?"

"No way. The only water I swim in is either a

heated pool or the Mediterranean. Besides, you're in charge of this excursion."

"Unfortunately true. Almost…there. Aha! Got…it!" He leaned way over, dangerously tipping the punt in the process, and managed to grab the pole, which disappointed Hope slightly. She wouldn't have minded seeing his clothes clinging to him if he'd had to get soaking wet.

With a triumphant whoop, he twisted to sit on the floor of the boat and raised the pole over his head like a victorious gladiator. That grin of his flashed wide as water dripped over his eyebrows and down his temples from the hair above his forehead, which had apparently gotten dipped into the river during the pursuit. Water dripped from his wet sleeves, too, and he looked so adorably boyish at that moment, her heart got disturbingly squishy.

"Impressed?" he asked as he rested the pole on his knees to wipe water from his face.

"Impressed that we whacked into the bank, nearly knocking us off our feet? That you might have had to swim for the pole or we'd be trapped in the middle of the river for days?"

"No." He moved to sit beside her. A few drops

of water dripped on her shirt when he moved to wrap his arm around her shoulder, until he must have realized how wet he was and rested it on his lap instead. He leaned close, his eyes gleaming. "Impressed that I managed to stop kissing you and touching you long enough to deal with the problem. Would have thought only a ten-magnitude earthquake would shake me out of that kind of trance."

"Oh." Apparently, he'd put her in a similar trance. And apparently she still was, since "oh" was the only word that came to mind.

"Besides, if we'd gotten stuck in the middle of the river, I would have gone into the water and towed you to safety. Just like Humphrey Bogart in *The African Queen*."

"I'd like to see that." The image had her giggling again. "Maybe I'll come punting with you again sometime after all."

"No maybe about it." He pressed his lips to hers and her humor faded as she clutched his wet sleeves, a part of her mind vaguely thinking that it wouldn't be such a bad thing to be trapped on a boat with him for days on end. Not a bad thing at all.

The boat lurched again, banging their mouths together. "Ouch!" Hope pressed her fingers to her lips, and he pulled them away, peering with a frown.

"You okay?"

"Yes. You?" She pressed her fingers to his lips and he smiled against them before kissing each one.

"No blood. Which is unfortunate, since a man like me enjoys bragging about sporting injuries." He stood and grabbed the pole, pushing them from the bank. "Even so, I'd better get this boat under control before we hit some wild rapids."

"There are no wild rapids on the River Cam."

"Are you sure? Because just being on it with you has felt like a wild ride, and I'm ready for more of it."

A wild ride. Being with Aaron was definitely that. Even as he steered the boat, his eyes kept returning to hers, holding so much heat that her skin warmed without even his touch. She didn't have to be a mind reader to know exactly what the man had "more of" in mind, and her breath caught.

Should she let herself have one more wild ride with him?

She watched his muscles bunch as he pushed the pole into the water, his wet sleeves outlining his forearms and biceps with every steady stroke. His gaze collided with hers, and she knew the answer.

Yes. This crazy attraction between them was like nothing she'd felt before. Aaron didn't want a relationship, and she didn't either. She'd spent her life being confident in what she wanted and acting on it, including her decision to get pregnant and start a family. She felt good about that. She did, except for those times she let the negative voices of her past drown out her optimism.

And right now, she felt good about Aaron Cartwright, too. She wanted him, and couldn't think of a single reason why she shouldn't act on it for one more doubtless amazing time.

Her future plans weren't a factor. They weren't his business or anyone else's. He'd move on and she'd have her new life and all would be wonderful.

"You still have that brandy in your apartment you offered me before?"

"I do." His brow arched over the super-heated gleam in his eyes. "You needing to be warmed up?"

"I am," she said softly, resolutely throwing all caution overboard. "I find I'm needing it very much."

CHAPTER SEVEN

"HERE." AARON WRAPPED Hope's slender fingers around the snifter, his mouth already watering just thinking about how it would taste on her tongue when he kissed her. "Liquid warmth."

"Mmm. Liquid warmth sounds nice."

It sure did. His breath backed up in his lungs at the way she looked up at him beneath her lashes, a sexy smile on her lips as she sipped the brandy. The kind of liquid warmth he wanted to get his fingers on—her own special brand of liquid warmth that another part of his body couldn't wait to enjoy again. A part currently throbbing so hard he could barely think.

He remembered to take a swallow of his own drink, thinking maybe he should chug it instead of sip it so they could move on fast to the next part of their evening together. It would burn his throat, but would doubtless be preferable to this burning desire for her that he could barely bank down.

"So tell me," he asked, partly because he wanted to know, and partly because he needed to ratchet back his libido before he pounced on her like a Rottweiler on a filet mignon. "Why did you decide you wanted to come here tonight, when you told me after the gala that you could only offer me one time together?"

"Because I realized short-term fun doesn't have to be limited to once." She set her glass on the bar and stepped close to wrap her arms around his neck, a smile in her beautiful eyes. "Twice seems like a good plan when it's you, which is why I decided to seduce you one last time."

"Was that you seducing me?" A short laugh came from his chest, despite the disturbing feeling her words "one last time" gave him. And why they felt disturbing was a complete mystery, since women who didn't want anything from him were exactly the kind he preferred to date. "Insulting a man's skill at sport is how you seduce him?"

"Well, honestly, I don't have a lot of experience in seduction, so I'm sorry if my technique was lacking." Her lips came against his in a featherlight touch. "Asking to come here for brandy was about as forward as I get."

"You don't need a single seduction technique, Hope," he whispered against the sweet lips touching his. "You seduced me the second I saw you at the gala. Hell, you seduced me every time I saw you at the hospital when we'd never even met."

"Sounds like we're on the same page, then. Mutual seduction for one more memorable night."

He looked deep into the sincere blue of her eyes, realizing she really meant that she wanted this to be it for them, and wondered if the peculiar, off-balance sensation that gave him was from the shoe being on the other foot this time, or from something else.

He carefully set his snifter on the bar, but before he could analyze what he was feeling Hope pressed her soft breasts to his chest and kissed him.

His eyes closed as her tongue licked across his lower lip, then swept inside to dance with his. Just as he'd guessed, the taste of the brandy in both their mouths added one more layer of tingling heat to their kiss. A kiss that held the same intense chemistry he'd felt with her that very first night roared through his blood, leaving him feeling dazed and crazed and more than a little out of control.

He grasped her shapely butt cheeks in his palms and lifted her, achingly sliding her body up his until it was right where he needed it to be. At first, he felt beyond grateful she responded by wrapping her legs tightly around his waist, until the pressure of her pelvis against his rock-hard body nearly undid him. He groaned into her mouth, and took a few steps to his biggest armchair before his legs buckled under him, sitting with her knees on either side of his hips.

"Time to enjoy some more of that liquid warmth," he managed to say as he found the elastic waist of her sweat pants and slid his hand inside.

"I left my brandy on the bar. I—oh, Aaron…"

He slipped his fingers farther inside her panties, loving the sound of his name on her lips. The sound of her moan. "This is the liquid warmth I've wanted all night. You, too?"

Her answer was unintelligible against his mouth, her breathing growing as ragged as his own. The soft slide of her mouth and tongue against his, the feel of her wet heat, was about to make him lose control, and he pulled his mouth from hers. Forced his hazy mind to focus on how he was touching her, on bringing her the pleasure she deserved. The pleasure he wanted so much to give.

The problem with that plan was that he was looking at her now. At her eyes, staring at him, slightly glassy but filled with desire, too. At her lips, moist, parted as she breathed. Just like that first night when he'd touched her like this, as his blood pounded through his veins and his heart drummed in his ears he was certain he'd never seen anything as beautiful as Hope Sanders about to climax.

He brought his other hand from her back to tunnel beneath her shirt and her bra, cupping her breast and caressing her nipple softly with his palm. "Come for me, Hope," he whispered, because he wanted to see her face when it happened, and because he was afraid if she didn't he damned well might and completely embarrass himself. "I want to be inside you, and—"

"I...we...oh..." Her voice trembled and shook with her body, and when she finally opened her eyes again, he expected that she might look a little self-conscious, just as she had their first night together. Instead she gave him a slow smile, then reached to press both palms to his beating heart, filling him with that sense of connection he kept feeling with her. Of belonging, which made no sense because he'd never really belonged anywhere. Had always known he never would.

"Aaron." She leaned forward to kiss him and he sank into the pleasure of it, surprised that after the intense heat of the past minutes the sensation felt more sweet and intimate than lustful. He held her face between his hands and made love to her mouth. Tunneled his fingers into the silky soft, golden waves that had been the very first thing he'd noticed about her long ago.

He had a feeling they would have sat that way for a long, blissful, strangely content moment if Hope hadn't broken the kiss to pull her shirt over her head. Slid from his lap to wriggle out of her athletic pants. She reached for his pants as she stood there, gorgeous and tantalizing, in only her bra and panties, and his breath got stuck in his lungs. "Time for these to come off, Dr. Cartwright. Ecstasy Street doesn't go only one way."

"You're the driver." Only too happy to strip fast, he had his clothes off in record time and pulled her underwear off, too. Picking her up to sit straddling his lap once more, he got distracted by the view. Her pink nipples on pert breasts, her smooth, pale shoulders, the slender curve of her waist and the moist triangle between her legs he'd had the privilege to touch only moments ago.

"You are so beautiful. I could look at you all night. Kiss you all night." It was true, and the first thing he wanted to kiss was that taut bit of pink candy right in front of him. He lowered his head to take her nipple into his mouth, but to his surprise she jerked back.

"Uh-uh. You gave me the driver's seat, remember?"

"Yeah. But the passenger's allowed to touch the music dial, right?"

Her eyes laughed at the same time they smoldered. "Maybe later." Her warm palms cupped his cheeks as she kissed him, then slid down to his chest and stomach, and every inch they traveled sent sparks across his flesh. He lifted his hands to her breasts, hoping like hell she wouldn't object, because he wanted to touch her, too, wanted to feel every inch of her soft skin.

After long minutes of kissing and touching until both were more than ready to move to the next step, he stood, carrying her in his arms as he strode to the bathroom to grab a condom. She took it from him with a smile so sensuous, it stole what little breath he had left. He realized at that moment there was nothing in the world more seductive than a sweet, smart woman who knew what she wanted both outside and inside the bedroom.

He dropped back down into the chair and groaned as she took charge of the condom, then lifted herself onto him. They moved slowly together, and the connection between them changed. More intimate, more overwhelming, as she moved on him. The look that had been on her face when he'd touched her was there again, her eyes intensely fixed on his as they moved in a rhythm as perfect and fulfilling as what they'd shared before. As he grasped her hips and made her one with him. As they moved together, building speed, until they peaked and crested and rounded the corner, flying across the finish line together.

Her silky hair spreading across his chest, her breath came hot against his chest as she collapsed onto him. He slowly stroked her back and beautiful round bottom, trying to get his breathing under control, feeling as blissed-out as he'd ever felt in his life. Then a peculiar sensation permeated the fog and his eyes sprang open in horror.

"Jesus, Hope." She lifted her head to look at him, clearly hearing the panic in his voice. "I think the condom broke."

Hope practically fell off his lap, all post-lovemaking deliciousness obliterated as Aaron jumped up, and the truth of his statement was instantly all too obvious. She looked up from the offending condom to see alarm all over Aaron's face.

"I'm so sorry. Damn it, this is…" He stopped and shook his head, his voice tight as he strode off to the bathroom to take care of the problem.

She wished she could reassure him that he didn't need to worry, but was afraid any conversation about her fertility issues would lead to things she didn't want to talk about. Like her plans for IVF and why, which were no one's business but hers.

But she could tell him she was at the wrong

time of her cycle, which was the truth. Except standing there naked with the bloom completely off the rose, so to speak, wasn't the time to have a conversation about anything. She grabbed up her underwear and bra, getting them on in record time before Aaron came back. He'd somehow donned his sweatpants again, and had a big navy blue robe in his hands that he held open for her.

"I don't know what to say," he said, a deep frown between his brows. "I just bought the damned things, so how that could have happened, I don't know."

She slipped into the robe and tugged it tightly around her, figuring she'd feel better if she covered up now and finished dressing later in private. "Well, the good news is I keep careful track of my cycle, and this isn't the time for anything to happen, so I'm positive we don't need to be worried about that."

"You're sure?" He looked at her from his bar where he'd picked up their brandy snifters again, placing them on a table next to the chair.

"I'm sure." Poor man was finally looking more normal, thank goodness. He'd blanched so white she'd thought he might pass out. Obviously, he was a man who had zero interest in being a father, but then again, nobody wanted an unexpected pregnancy from a fling, anyway, right? But his distress was the perfect reason to emphasize again that they couldn't go out anymore, and she had a feeling that this time he'd agree.

She couldn't allow that thought to make her feel slightly blue.

"I probably should head on home now. I assume you're willing to give me a lift? Or do I need to ride my bike home?" she said jokingly, resolutely squashing the inconvenient regret suddenly poking at her heart over never seeing him again.

"Funny." He closed the gap between them to grasp her elbows. A fairly loud breath of obvious relief whooshed from his lungs as he kissed her forehead. "Sorry I freaked out, but I figured you'd be upset, too. If you're not worried, though, that's good."

Not worried about the broken condom, but about him finding out about her IVF plans? For whatever reason, the thought still made her very uncomfortable, no matter how confident and good she felt about that decision.

"No worries. Honest." She tugged loose from his hold and leaned over to pick up her clothes again, squeaking in surprise when he swept her up into his arms and sat back down in the chair.

"I'll take you home soon, but I want to feel your warm body curved in my lap just a little longer," he said, touching his lips to her forehead and folding her close against him. "All right?"

"All right." And it was. More than all right. His firm chest and soft skin felt like the perfect place to rest her head, and she let herself relax into the rare comfort of being held like this. "So tell me more about your adoption foundation," Hope murmured, since she'd been wondering but hadn't asked yet. Apparently too distracted by all the kissing and lovemaking they'd done since practically the moment they'd met. "I heard you've got another Christmas party scheduled for it?"

"Next Wednesday. The hotel where we held the fund-raising gala is giving me a good price on one of their meeting rooms, and my office staff is decorating it."

"More fund-raising with a different crowd?"

"No. This one is to give parents wanting to adopt a chance to meet children in a casual, fun environment. And for the kids to meet them, too, without the pressure and nervousness that can come with one-on-one introductions."

His hands slowly moved on her, up and down her arm, stroking her neck, cupping her jaw, twining his fingers with hers, and a fuzzy tenderness filled her heart. She'd been touched before. She was thirty-four-years old, for heaven's sake. Why did it feel so different, so overwhelming, with this man?

Probably because her plans to have a baby, to change her life, had given her a reason to relax around him. To not worry about what she could or couldn't give. A sense of freedom, she supposed, since all the usual dynamics of dating didn't apply anymore.

"That's such a great idea," she said, trying to focus on the conversation without getting distracted. Impressed all over again at how caring he was, how multifaceted. "Really wonderful—I can just picture all the children and adults enjoying spending time together, but with an important purpose, too."

"It works well. Everyone eats together and plays

games, and with any luck find a good fit they want to pursue."

"Do you need some help? I did a lot of babysitting as a teen—babies are so adorable, it's what made me decide to become a midwife. But I enjoy all children, and I know quite a few games that would be fun to play."

"That would be great." He smiled down at her, pressing his lips to her nose. "I'm jealous I never had a babysitter like you. I can easily picture you as the cutest, most popular babysitter a kid could want."

Why did everything he said make her heart feel absurdly warm and squishy? They were just words, the kind a man like Aaron flirted and teased with, but she couldn't help but like hearing them anyway. "I'll plan on it, then."

The second the words were out of her mouth, she froze. Tonight was clear evidence that she couldn't resist his charms whenever they spent time together, even when she planned to. What was she thinking? She was about to start her fertility treatments. Any more time with him was out of the question.

Panic welled up as her mind spun, trying to find

a plausible excuse to back out of her ill-thought-out commitment, at the same time wishing she could help such a great cause. Then grinned at the "eureka" solution that struck her. Unwitting chaperones.

"I'll ask one or two of the midwives at the hospital if they'd like to come along, too," she said. Surely that would help both of them stay at arm's length, wouldn't it?

"Any and all help is welcome."

He didn't seem to interpret her suggestion for what it really was, and she relaxed. "So, I've been wondering what made you decide to start the foundation. I know it had to have taken a lot of work."

He focused his attention on her hair, lazily twirling it between his fingers for so long, she wondered if he'd even heard her question. She was about to open her mouth to ask again, when he finally spoke.

"I was adopted, and my parents gave me a good home and upbringing. In California, I did a little volunteering with a great organization that helps children become permanently placed with families, instead of moving around for years from one home to another in foster care. When I came to Cambridge and saw the same challenges older children had in finding real homes, I decided I'd like to bring that model here."

"How old were you when you were adopted?"

Again the silence. Since it didn't seem like a particularly troubling question, she had to wonder what, exactly, his history was that he clearly didn't like to talk about. Finally, he gave her a short answer. "It wasn't an issue for me, but it is for a lot of kids."

Another oddly evasive response. She swiveled in his arms a little, trying to see his eyes, which were still focused on her hair. "Not an issue for you?"

Finally, his eyes met hers again. She couldn't interpret what was in them, exactly, but was that pain she saw deep inside?

She cupped his cheek in her hand. "You can tell me, you know. Just between us, I promise."

He stared at her a long moment, his face impassive, and just when she'd become sure he wouldn't share anything with her, he spoke. "I was almost two when I went into foster care. My biological mother was...unstable. Children's Services gives a parent as much time as they can to get healthy, but it didn't happen. My parents adopted me when I was seven."

"Oh, Aaron." Her heart hurt for the little boy he used to be, having to leave his mother then moving from home to home for years until he found a family. "That sounds...very hard. But you do know, don't you, how impressive it is that you've taken a difficult experience and turned it into a positive? Starting your foundation to help children and parents find one another is a wonderful thing."

He pulled her close and pressed his lips to hers, making it very obvious he didn't want to talk about it anymore. That the subject was over. The pinch in her heart from learning about the past pain in his life faded as his mouth moved on hers. Kissing her with such softness, such unbearable sweetness, she found herself unable to think about anything but the way he made her feel as she melted into him all over again.

"How about your issues?" he whispered against her lips. "Why are you so damned determined to have a specific, preplanned expiration date for us, starting tomorrow?"

She opened her eyes to look into the brown ones meeting hers again, no longer seemingly evasive, but very, very serious. And that seriousness nearly pulled the truth out of her. Nearly made her want to come clean, and that would be that and she wouldn't have to worry about him finding out, worry about how he'd react, any more.

But she couldn't, even though she probably should. Didn't want to see whatever his reaction would be. He'd given her only the bare bones of his own history though, right? She could give him the same thing. Not the painful distance between her parents that had made their home life uncomfortable. Not her father's obvious resentment of being stuck with her and her mum, which was doubtless part of her inability to love a man.

She'd share some of her history. But her future? That, she'd keep to herself. The future she both worried about and couldn't wait for.

"I dated a man for a long time. Eight years, and I still didn't want to commit. Just couldn't. So he broke it off. Never met anyone afterward I wanted anything permanent with, either, so I realized I must just not be cut out for something like that."

"That answers the question that's been bothering me, which is how the amazing Hope Sanders could possibly still be single." He placed his fingers beneath her chin, bringing her gaze back to his, which she hadn't even realized she'd moved to the wall behind him. "But I don't get what that has to do with us dating a little while. Two people, neither wanting a permanent relationship, who have enough electricity between them to light the entire city of Cambridge. Sounds pretty perfect to me."

Well, darn. She should have realized her answer wouldn't work, because he'd already said he had no interest in permanency, either.

"My life just isn't in a place where I can date you or anyone." She forced a light tone to her voice to banish the serious turn the conversation had taken. "But for what it's worth, if it was, you'd be at the top of the list. And I'd like to leave it at that, okay?"

Solemn brown eyes studied her face for what seemed like long minutes before he nodded.

"Still interested in helping with the party? If not, I won't hold you to it."

"Of course I'll still help with the party. What

better way to celebrate the Christmas season than helping children find good homes?"

"Thank you." He leaned forward to press his lips to hers, and she soaked in their sweetness, trying to ignore the sharp sting in her chest that it had to be their very last kiss. "I'll leave the agenda on the front desk at the office so you can see what we already have planned."

"Okay." She set down her glass and slid off his lap, grabbing up her clothes. "I'd better be going. I have an early day at the hospital tomorrow."

She didn't look back as she hurried to the bathroom, but knew he watched her go. Could feel his eyes on her every bit as painfully as she could feel the tight pinch in her heart that this was really goodbye.

CHAPTER EIGHT

"So THE PARTY is tomorrow, Bonnie, and I was wondering if you had any interest in helping me conduct some games for the children and potential parents," Hope said over the tea she and the energetic new midwife were sharing in the hospital cafeteria. "A few other people from the hospital will be there, and some of the parents coming have other children. I thought it might be a fun way for you to meet people."

"Sounds really nice, Hope. How sweet of you to think of me!" Bonnie smiled. "What a wonderful thing, a Christmas party to bring children together with people looking to adopt. I don't know Dr. Cartwright, other than that he's dreamily good-looking, but he's now high on my list of wonderful people at CRMU."

On Hope's, too, but she wasn't about to say so. Also had to stop thinking about the dreamily good-looking man. The man who wasn't only dreamy, but an amazing doctor, a caring man. With eyes like warm fudge and a crooked smile you couldn't help but smile back at.

How could she have fallen under the man's spell after spending mere hours with him? Clearly she wasn't cut out to have quick flings, if she couldn't stop feeling all gooey about him when it was over with. Who would have known she was even capable of that? But since that was the undeniable truth, she so wished she hadn't agreed to help with his party.

Somehow, she'd have to avoid him as much as possible by concentrating on the children and talking with Bonnie and the other CRMU staff instead of gazing like a schoolgirl at Dr. Aaron Cartwright.

"Yes, his adoption foundation is doing a lot of good." She tried to keep her voice professional, without a hint that thinking of the way the man kissed and made love kept invading her brain every time she mentioned him, sending unwelcome heat across her skin. Which instantly turned icy when she thought of her appointment this afternoon, and how she'd have to make sure she stealthily avoided Aaron Cartwright like a cat burglar while she was there. "I'll be picking up the party agenda from his office, and you and I can see what might fit into it."

"Could I bring my daughter, Freya?"

"I don't see why not. She'd probably have lots of fun. How old is she?"

"Just five. But fun is her middle name, believe me."

"Five is such an adorable age. I can't wait to meet her. And since I'm sure you have lots of experience playing games with Freya, it'll be wonderful to have you play with the children her age at the party, too. I'm so glad you can come." Hope drank the last of her tea, swallowing down the sick feeling in the pit of her stomach at the thought of heading to the offices the IVF doctors shared. "Got to go. Thanks for helping. See you tomorrow."

Hands sweating, she hurried down the hallway to meet with Dr. Devor. She stood outside the closed door, thinking the heavy, dark wood looked grimly ominous, then nearly laughed slightly hysterically at the ridiculous thought. Was she being overdramatic or what? She sucked in a great gulp of fortifying air and stepped inside.

The receptionist took her promptly back to a different waiting room, and she dropped into the chair, her knees a little weak with relief. How could she have gotten so lucky to have been whisked out of the waiting room so fast? Hidden from brown eyes that would doubtless have held a very big question.

Stop this right now, she scolded herself. She was more than ready to begin the IVF treatments. She could not allow herself to worry about anything, or what anyone thought, especially a man she'd simply slept with and was now not going to see ever again except at one little Christmas party and from afar at the hospital. If he found out, so be it. She'd hold her head up proudly and be the person she'd always been, a woman who knew what she wanted and went for it.

Despite her big, brave pep talk, her heart leaped into her throat at the short knock on the door before it opened. "Dr. Devor!" She knew her voice sounded overly enthused, the relieved smile on her face so wide the man probably thought she was slightly nutty.

"Hope. Good to see you," he said with a smile as he shut the door behind him. "I'm sorry I wasn't here for your appointment last week. My son at university was in a car accident, and my wife and I had to go see him in the hospital."

"Oh, no. Is he all right?"

"Thankfully, yes. Banged his noggin pretty good, though. I told him he was lucky to be so hardheaded."

"That sounds like the kind of thing my father likes to say to me, too. Stubbornness is a virtue, as far as I'm concerned."

He chuckled as he sat in a chair in front of hers. "I agree, along with determination, which I've seen that you have in abundance. Did you go through all the literature I sent home with you?"

"I did. I've been thoroughly educating myself on all of it." The procedure didn't scare her. It was everything else twisting her stomach in a knot.

"Good." He nodded. "It's unfortunate we weren't successful with intrauterine insemination. It's likely due to your endometriosis, though I'd hoped it would still work. Have you thought about all we discussed regarding IVF and single parenting? The pros and cons?"

"I've thought about it very carefully and discussed everything at length with my parents." Her mum, at least, and she was fully behind Hope's decision. "I know what I'm getting into, and my family will help me as needed. I've wanted to be a mother forever, and I'm ready to do this."

"All right, then." He smiled. "I have every reason to believe that IVF will give you the baby you want."

The baby she wanted. A lump stuck in her throat as she had an instant vision of a cherub-faced infant, gurgling and cooing. A toddler running through her small house, eventually tired enough to snuggle in her lap. Growing into a child happily playing and reading books and giving abundant love and hugs, and it all filled her chest with such an overwhelming joy, she knew she had to be making the right decision. Having a job she adored and, when she wasn't working, holding a baby of her own in her arms? Perfect and wonderful.

She clasped her hands and drew a fortifying breath. "So let's get started."

"Here's the schedule we'll follow." He handed her a calendar. "Today we'll draw your blood to do some necessary tests. When you come back next week, you'll receive an injection of FSH, which is a hormone that will stimulate your ovaries to produce more than one egg. The following week, we'll do some more blood tests and use ultrasound to determine if the eggs are ready for collection. If not, we'll need to give the FSH a little more time to work, usually just another day or two, then you'll get an injection of a medication that will help the eggs ripen."

"And then you'll retrieve the eggs?"

"Timing is important. We can't take them out too soon, or too late, or they won't develop normally." Maybe he saw the worry she couldn't help feel, because he smiled and leaned forward to pat her knee. "I've got it down to a science, I promise. And you'll be sedated when I retrieve the eggs at the perfect time."

"I know. I got to see Dr. Cartwright retrieving a patient's eggs and it was pretty amazing." Saying his name brought that awful twisting feeling to her belly again, which was beyond irritating. Why did that keep happening? He had nothing to do with her life or her goals or her future.

"Dr. Cartwright is very good at his job, and I am, too. You saw there's nothing to be scared about." Another smile from Dr. Devor. "So as we discussed on your first appointment, the eggs I retrieve will meet the donor sperm right away. We'll keep an eye on them while they spend a few days together, then I'll look to see which three seem the most viable, and freeze the rest that look good. Then we'll be ready for the IVF."

"You said that's done pretty quickly, right?"

He nodded. "Usually takes only about half an hour. Most women find it virtually painless. Resuming your normal activity is absolutely fine, just no vigorous exercise. Then we wait to see if one or more of the three eggs implants into the uterine wall."

Nervous and excited butterflies flapped around in her belly. "We'll know in about a week and a half, then?"

"Hopefully, though if we don't have a positive pregnancy test at that time we give it another few days and check again."

"Okay." She expelled a big breath and smiled. "I'd like to get started on the stimulating hormones as soon as possible."

"I got a little backed up from being gone, and I apologize for that. But the receptionist will fit you into my schedule as early as possible next week, and we'll have all the lab results in plenty of time before you come."

"All right." Next week suddenly seemed like an eternity, but she stuffed down her impatience. She did a quick mental calculation of the timing for taking the meds and the time needed after the procedure and had to smile. Maybe this delay was meant to be. Maybe learning she was pregnant was going to be the best Christmas present she'd ever had.

As she scheduled her next appointment her mind spun with the thrill of it all. A large envelope with her name on it caught her eye at the receptionist desk, and she remembered Aaron had said he'd leave the party agenda at the front desk for her.

Which brought her to earth with a hard thud, and started those nerves flapping all over again. She furtively glanced around the office, praying she wouldn't see him. Yes, she was as confident as she could be under the circumstances, beyond happy about this next phase of her life, but she didn't feel like talking about it with anyone yet, least of all the man she'd had hot sex with just days ago.

"So you're all set for next Thursday," the receptionist said, looking at her a little quizzically. "We'll see you then."

She flushed, wondering what her expression had been as the thought of Aaron and hot sex and the fear of seeing him had swept through her brain. "Great. Thanks. And I think that envelope is for me."

"Oh. So it is."

She handed it to Hope, who hightailed it out of there, beyond relieved that she'd again dodged running into Aaron. Their time together was too fresh for that, but surely, after enough months had passed for her pregnancy to show, their brief fling would seem very distant, long ago and unimportant.

Except it felt all too disturbingly important right then, and she had a bad feeling it would for a long time.

The sight of silky blond waves tumbling down the back of a tall, slender woman had Aaron doing a double take as he stepped from his office to the front desk, and his heart kicked sharply in his chest. He didn't have to see her sweet face to recognize every gentle curve of Hope Sanders. The door to the hallway closed behind her, and he had a sudden urge to run after her.

But of course he wouldn't. Their relationship had been a brief and memorable moment in time. Fantastic while it lasted, but over with whether he liked it or not.

She must have come into the office to get the party agenda. He looked down at the desktop and, sure enough, the envelope was gone.

The odd weight in his chest lifted a little that he'd at least get to see her at the party. He knew whatever she came up with for the kids to do would be a big hit. Also knew he had to stop thinking about her, but the good news was his work didn't bring him to the labor and delivery suites very often. His memories of her would fade, and this disturbing preoccupation would fade along with them.

Looking for a new job should probably happen soon. If he decided to move on, his memories of Hope would surely fade even faster, and the thought held both appeal and melancholy. He realized he'd miss Cambridge and the CRMU, which took him a little by surprise.

"When is my next patient scheduled?" he asked Sue as she sent the receptionist on her break and settled herself in the desk chair.

"Um…" she responded, peering at the computer screen. "In fifteen minutes. Plenty of time for you to grab more coffee."

"Just had a cup. I'll stay here and bother you instead."

"Or you could man the desk while I file these and go grab a quick nap," she said, picking up the stack of patient folders on the desk.

"Right. Whirling tornados don't nap, which is why the staff gets out of your way when you barrel through. You—" He stopped mid-word when he saw the folder at the top of Sue's stack. A folder with the name Hope Sanders on it.

"What is that file?" he asked, tapping it with his finger. "She's single. A midwife here."

"I know." Sue glanced at him, then quickly stacked some more files on top of the pile. "She's the woman you were dancing with in the newspaper photo. The one you denied you had any interest in."

Yeah, and he was still going to. And didn't have any interest, really, because she didn't and it was over. "I don't. I'm just confused why there would be a file for her here unless she's a patient."

"Well, you're a doctor in this office. You want to look at the file, you have the right to, but I'm staying out of it."

The frown between her brows, the way she was warily looking at him like the bearer of bad news, sent alarm bells clanging in his brain. Which was stupid, since he didn't have a relationship with Hope Sanders. But as he was trying to convince himself of that, he dug through the stack for it, slid it out and flipped it open.

There was the usual column with the dates patients were in the office, then the next column listing the doctor they'd seen. Two appointments with Tom Devor were noted. The most recent being today. Along with Tom's summary notes on her visit, and the scheduled hormone injections to begin next week, preparing her for IVF.

He blinked, feeling as if the room were tilting a little, then somehow refocused on the page. The scrawled notes practically jumped off the page, loud and clear and unbelievable.

Hope was going to have IVF. The woman he'd kissed and touched and made unforgettable love with just days ago wanted to get pregnant and have a baby from some anonymous sperm donor who wouldn't have one damned thing to do with his child's life. The kid would forever wonder who he was and where he came from and why.

At first utterly numb, his whole body started to feel as if a million little needles were jabbing it, from his feet to the prickle of his scalp, and it got a little hard to breathe. His gaze moved from the file in his hand to Sue. To see the twist of her lips and concern in her eyes that told him she knew all about it, and also knew his claims to not be interested in the woman had been a damned lie.

"Maybe you should sit down for a minute," Sue said, her frown deepening as she stood. "Use this chair."

"I'm fine." And he damned well would be, as soon as he told Hope exactly what he thought about a single woman becoming a parent through IVF, risking multiple births and the potential terrible consequences of that. Yeah, he knew it was none of his business. He wasn't her doctor and he wasn't her boyfriend, and now he saw loud and clear why she'd insisted they couldn't go out again.

Because she'd likely be pregnant very soon.

How was it possible that a beautiful woman like Hope Sanders wanted to have a baby, or multiple babies, all alone? Surely, there was a line of men who'd love nothing more than to have a permanent relationship with her and have a family.

He sucked in a shaky breath, trying to wrap his brain around the whole thing as he seriously pondered heading to her house the second he was off work to talk to her about it.

Sticking his nose in her business probably wouldn't be welcomed, because he was sure she believed she'd carefully thought about it all before deciding on this path. Nearly everyone always did. But he had personal experience with the subject, personal knowledge of how negatively the challenges could affect both her and her children. Challenges that sometimes brought terrible consequences and lifelong pain.

Your mother has given up her parental rights, Aaron. And you know, of course, that we don't know who your father is. I understand all this might make you feel sad, but it's for the best. It means you can find a permanent family to live with, just like your brother and sister have. It's going to be okay.

His fingers tightened on the folder until they were white. Didn't he have an obligation to warn Hope that there was no way she was fully aware of what she and her babies could be facing? Wasn't that why he'd decided to become a fertility specialist to begin with, so he could make sure patients wanting a family truly knew all the pros and cons of IVF? Especially when the doctor performing the procedure was perfectly okay with implanting more than two eggs?

He hated that his hand was shaking as he carefully set Hope's file with the others. "I'll be in my office when my patient arrives."

"I'm sorry this is upsetting to you, Aaron," Sue said, reaching to touch his forearm.

"It's not upsetting. Just surprising. I barely know the woman." Which was obviously true, since he never would have dreamed she had anything like this in mind.

He dropped into his desk chair, wishing he still had paperwork left to do. Hoped like hell his patients came early. Focusing on them would be the distraction he needed to shove down the shock and disbelief he knew he shouldn't be feeling so intensely. Probably talking to Hope about it would be wrong. Probably by the end of the day his intense desire to run to her house that minute would fade away, and he'd be feeling more normal.

Which unfortunately didn't happen. By the end of the work day his shock had faded, but his need to talk to her about it hadn't. He tried to convince himself that the only interest he had in Hope's decision was professional but knew that was a lie.

He'd wondered why she'd been so adamant about them not going out more than once or twice. Now that he knew the reason, he should be glad it didn't have anything to do with him. Shrug, and let it go. But the truth was, the thought of her getting pregnant through IVF without any support, without a man in her life, without a father for her children, twisted him up in knots.

But as he'd reminded himself ten times in the past few hours, her life was none of his business. He couldn't let it be, and forcefully stuffed down his consuming urge to show up at her door to talk to her, which would be completely inappropriate.

If she ended up coming to the Christmas adoption party to help, he'd be friendly but distant.

After that, he'd rarely run into her, unless he was unlucky enough to be in the office the same time she saw Tom Devor. It would be easy to not notice the blue of her eyes. Not notice that gorgeous hair cascading down her back or tamed into a ponytail. Not notice her appealing body in the hallway at the hospital, a body that would change as it carried multiple babies. To not take a second look at her in the cafeteria, smiling and laughing with coworkers, or be aware of her absence when she was on maternity leave.

He grabbed up his briefcase and headed out of the door, deciding the longest run he'd ever taken might be the cure to this jittery, unsettled feeling that wouldn't leave his gut.

Hope Sanders had her life and the decisions she'd made for it, and he had his, which would never include a family. It would be easy to forget all about her.

It would.

CHAPTER NINE

IT WAS SCHEDULED. It was going to happen.

The thought fluttered around Hope's head and heart, taking center stage every time there was a lull at work. Nervousness warred with the excitement in her belly every time she thought of her meeting with Dr. Devor, wondering how the hormones would feel, how they might affect her, what it would be like to have her eggs retrieved once they were ready. Thinking about the fertilization, and how long the week or two would drag on as the cells grew. Thinking about having them implanted into her uterus.

Thinking about really and truly becoming pregnant.

"Congratulations. What a beauty," she said to the awestruck new parents of the baby she'd just helped bring into the world as she placed it, warm and swaddled, into its mother's arms. She hoped her smile showed only her sincerity and didn't at all reveal how antsy she felt about her own life now that she had a moment to think about it all again. "I'll leave the three of you alone for a bit, then I'll be back."

She left the labor and delivery room, wiping her suddenly sweaty hands against her scrubs, wanting to give the thrilled couple some privacy to enjoy their incredibly special first moment with their newborn baby. Maybe a nice, hot cup of tea would calm the restlessness she felt that was more than uncomfortable.

Almost every woman pregnant, or expecting to become pregnant, for the first time felt as she did, didn't they? Elated at the thought of becoming a mother, but a little worried about the rest of it? Wondering about how her body would change, about how the delivery would go, about whether she'd have an infant that slept through the night in just weeks, or one that had colic and cried all the time, even one who might have some developmental difficulty?

Regardless, it didn't matter. The baby or babies she'd be blessed to mother would be all hers, for better or worse, easy or difficult or anywhere in between. She was absolutely sure she could handle whatever came her way, and the thought helped her relax. As did picturing her mum as a very happy grandma, coddling the little ones they'd been blessed with.

The vision brought a smile and she drew a deep breath, shaking her head at herself. Her mother might have had Hope far before she was ready, but she did love children. That kind of love had nothing to do with sensual love, the love between a man and woman. Hope might not have grown up seeing that, or personally experienced it, but knew they were totally separate things, and shoved down the fears and doubts that kept surfacing.

It would be fine. It would be wonderful, and the days until she saw Dr. Devor again to begin the process were going to seem very long indeed.

A distraction was in order, and the best distraction she could think of was checking on the babies she'd delivered that week, and their mothers. All were doing well, and she enjoyed the satisfaction of seeing thriving babies and happy families.

She made her way to the room where Mrs. Smith was recovering from her emergency C-section, pleased to see that her baby was there with

her, too. The woman looked tired, and no wonder, considering everything she'd been through,
but her smile was happy. "You look like you're
getting along pretty well, Mrs. Smith! And so is
baby. What did you name him?"

"Patrick. After his grandfather. Dr. Cartwright
told my Ted that our Patrick was such a 'bruiser'
he was sure to play rugby someday. Since his
granddad played rugby, we decided it was perfect.
Except now, his granddad is proudly calling him
'Bruiser' instead, so I'm afraid it just might stick."

"Patrick is a lovely name, but Bruiser is unique,
that's for sure." Hope had to chuckle, and for a
moment she saw not the mother and baby, but
Aaron. His eyes crinkling at the corners as he
spoke to Mr. Smith, coining that name for the
big baby who'd been very difficult to deliver.
Aaron had been incredibly calm and efficient
during the crisis delivery, especially considering he hadn't done it for a long time. And never
alone, which she was surprised he'd admitted,
and which showed his utter confidence in himself. The whole thing was amazing, really, and
she wondered if the parents had any idea how

lucky they'd all been that Aaron had been in the right place at the right time.

"Thank you for helping me and Patrick, Hope." Mrs. Smith reached to squeeze her hand. "I was terrified, so scared for the baby and for myself, too, I admit it. Dr. Cartwright told me the reason he's all right is because you knew right away what the problem was and got immediate help. We owe you a lot for that."

"You don't owe me anything. I'm so lucky my job gives me a chance to help mums and babies. And we're all lucky Dr. Cartwright was there to take charge and get Patrick delivered fast—he did an amazing job with a difficult situation. It's too bad you had to have a C-section, but I know having a healthy baby is well worth the pain you're going through recovering from it." Something she very well might have to experience, too, if more than one baby implanted from the IVF.

"More than worth it." She looked down at Patrick and smiled. "I understand that the kind of C-section I had to have means any more babies would have to be delivered the same way, but I'm okay with that as well. Babies are worth anything we have to go through, don't you think?"

"Yes, Mrs. Smith. I do." And she was about to go through quite a bit for hers, knowing her upcoming pregnancy would be her only pregnancy. She reached to stroke Patrick's downy head, getting another lump in her throat as she pictured holding her own in her arms in the not too distant future.

A quick knock came just before the sound of a familiar voice. "How are you and Bruiser doing today, Mrs. Smith?"

Hope stiffened and turned, knowing without a doubt who'd come in. Willing herself to act and feel normal, and not at all breathless and starry-eyed as she always seemed to be whenever he was near.

Aaron stopped dead in his tracks as their eyes met, his brows lowering in a deep frown. There was something about his expression that sent her heart pounding, and not in a good way. Something about the way his lips had thinned, the way his eyes narrowed slightly as he stared at her. Something about his stiff posture combined with all the rest of it seemed to be sending serious anger vibes directly at her, and her throat suddenly felt a little dry.

What had she done that had obviously disturbed him? Could he...? Surely he hadn't found out about her IVF plans? It must be something else. Something she couldn't think of at that moment. Or maybe she was completely imagining it.

Except the anxious quivers inside her gut didn't think she was imagining it at all.

"Ms. Sanders," he said in a voice that was tight and cool and unlike anything she'd heard from him before. "Nice to see you checking on our patients. If you have a minute, there's something I'd like to talk to you about after I've visited with the Smiths."

She nearly said, *Sorry, I can't,* because the alarm in her brain was ringing loud and clear that whatever he wanted to talk about wouldn't be a pleasant conversation. But avoiding it wouldn't be very mature or professional, and if it was something to do with her work she needed to know. Besides, she was a grown woman who could deal with anything thrown at her. "All right. I'll meet you in the hallway."

She turned to Mrs. Smith and forced a smile. "I'll come back tomorrow to see how you're doing, and with any luck you can take Patrick home soon."

Hope barely heard Mrs. Smith's response as she walked past Aaron to the door. He didn't even look at her as she did, moving to the side of the bed to talk to their patient, as though Hope were suddenly invisible.

What in the world? Out in the hallway, she sucked in a breath as the cowardly part of her urged her to leave, pointing out that if what Aaron wanted to talk about was important he'd find her later. But the perplexed and unnerved part of her wanted to know what was going on with him and get it over with.

She stood immobile for what was probably only minutes but seemed like an eternity, when the door finally swung open and Aaron was there. With the same confusing and disturbing expression on his face.

"Is there somewhere on this floor we can talk privately?"

Privately. Because of patient confidentiality, or because he was going to let loose on her for something? "There's a meeting room down this hall," she said, moving toward it, proud that her voice sounded pretty normal.

He followed, silent, closing the meeting room door behind them. Last thing she wanted to do was sit at the table for some long chat, so she stopped just a few steps into the room. Curls of foreboding rolled in her stomach as she faced him. "What did you want to talk about?"

Standing maybe three feet from her, he stared at her, folding his arms across his wide chest. The lights in the room were fluorescent, unforgiving, and seemed to emphasize the tension in his face, the harsh planes of it. "Yesterday, I was at the front desk at my office. Imagine my surprise when I saw a file there with your name on it."

So he did know. That was what this was about. She wiped her sweaty hands down her scrubs, fiercely reminding herself it didn't matter. He'd have learned about it sooner or later, and she didn't owe him a thing anyway. She tipped up her chin and waited.

"Why the hell are you going to do IVF? With Tom Devor, who doesn't worry about the possible ramifications of multiple births? Don't you realize the serious problems you could be bringing to both yourself and your children?"

"First, I've thought this through very carefully and am well aware of all the pluses and potential minuses. Second, I don't see how this is any of your business. Our relationship was brief, and now it's over."

"And now I know why." His eyes flashed at her. "What I don't know is why you're doing this. It may not be any of my business, but, since it's what I do for a living, I'm making it my business. You have plenty of time to find someone who would be a real father to your children and conceive naturally."

"Sorry, my reasons are not your concern, no matter what you do for a living." She didn't have to explain her mother's infertility from endometriosis when she was only in her twenties. Didn't have to tell him about her own early stages of the disease that would likely make conceiving harder as she got older. Didn't have to share her private inadequacies as a woman.

"Hope." He closed the gap between them to grasp her arms. "Believe me when I say I've been down this road too often, seeing single mothers without support who end up with twins or triplets or even more and can't handle it. They suffer and their babies suffer. Not to mention that many children who never had a father always, always wonder who he was. Always feel an emptiness, a deep longing to know where they came from and who they really are. Is that what you want for your children?"

She stared at him. At what could only be described as anguish along with the anger on his face. Obviously, he must have experienced the heartache he described because of his adoption history. Knowing he must carry some kind of deep pain about it, she felt her own anger at his attitude, at his apparent belief that he had a right to lecture her and tell her what to do, fade a little.

She pressed her palm against his chest and could feel his heart pounding. "I have good support, Aaron. My mum is excited about being a grandmother. She'll be there for me and my baby. Close ties with grandparents will fill any small gap a child feels—I'm sure of it. After all, there are millions of children with only one parent."

"And so many children with no parents, looking for a home." His voice had lowered, the angry tone tempered, but his eyes were still sharp, hard. "You can't count on your mother being here to help. Life has a way of destroying the things you count on. My own parents died just a year apart, both unexpectedly. Did it ever occur to you that you're being selfish? What if you were juggling your job and three babies, and the people helping were gone in an instant? What would you do then?"

"I'd figure it out." She pulled away from his hands, wanting to be done. Wanting to get away from his anger and deep disapproval, which painfully stabbed at her even though she shouldn't let it. "I appreciate that you must know patients who have had difficult problems. But a person can't just stop living because they might experience some challenges they didn't expect."

"I want you to cancel your appointment. Take more time to think about it. If you end up still wanting a child, you should consider adopting. Most already have abandonment issues, and they need a loving home they can call their own. And having one child wouldn't overwhelm you. A single parent."

"So you think I just couldn't handle more than

one, is that it? That I'm being *selfish*, thinking only about myself until the going gets tough?" Her own anger was back now, times ten. He'd said so many beautiful things to her, complimentary things, things that she'd thought meant he truly respected her. It had obviously just been part of the have-a-fling game she wasn't experienced with. But now she sure was and would never make that mistake again. "Who do you think you are, telling me what to do and what not to do? You don't even know me. And this conversation is over."

"Hope, listen, I—"

She shouldered past him, ignoring the way his voice had softened, ignoring the confusion and maybe even remorse in it. "Goodbye, Dr. Cartwright. Please stay out of my life."

Aaron parked his car, then just sat there with his head against the seat back. He always looked forward to the adoption party. Enjoyed talking with everyone having a nice time, observing and encouraging good fits between kids and adults that looked very promising for a future together.

But not this one. Feeling like an ass and a jerk,

and having to face the person he'd been an ass and jerk to, had him seriously considering skipping it this year.

Which of course he couldn't do. He owed it to the children hoping for a real family to show up and help them feel at ease. He owed it to the parents who'd been invited to talk with him about various ways the foundation supported them before and after adoption. And damn it, he owed it to Hope Sanders to show up and apologize to her.

He sat there a few more minutes, gathering the guts to walk inside. Hope was probably still mad as hell about the way he'd confronted her and lectured her, and who wouldn't be?

How had it happened, anyway? For the hundredth time, he inwardly thrashed himself about his loss of control. After his initial shock of learning Hope's plans had passed, he'd been sure he'd shoved it aside as none of his business. Yes, he liked Hope, but what she did with her life wasn't his concern. His own history didn't give him the right to lecture people on their choices, and even being a fertility doctor only gave him the right to give advice to his own patients. Not try to dictate their decisions.

But in spite of knowing all that, what had happened? The moment he'd walked into Mrs. Smith's room to see Hope's tender smile as she touched the baby's head, the reality that she was about to have the IVF procedure and get pregnant had punched him in the gut all over again, nearly knocking him flat.

Anger and frustration had welled up in his chest, consuming and overpowering. All common sense had been completely smothered out by bad memories. By the pain of his mother's mental illness. The pain of her abandonment. The pain of never knowing anything about his biological father and what kind of man he was.

It had fueled a burning need to tell her she was being crazy, that she had no idea of the horrible things that might happen, that she didn't understand the suffering she might unknowingly cause herself and her offspring.

So he'd blasted her with both barrels. And her reaction had been predictable. The way he would have reacted if someone had butted uninvited into his business and told him something he planned to do, wanted to do, would completely mess up his life and others along with it.

He heaved a deep sigh. He'd made plenty of mistakes in his life, done a few embarrassing things over the years, but this one was without a doubt one of the biggest. Hope probably assumed he was some macho man who believed he could boss women around, and her thinking of him that way sent a sick feeling to his gut.

He had to apologize. Probably, though, the only way she'd accept it, understand why he'd unleashed his verbal fury on her, was if he told her all of his history.

Which wasn't going to happen. His late parents were the only ones who'd known, and it was just as well that information had died with them.

He shoved open his car door and headed into the hotel, his legs feeling a little lead-like. No choice but to accept that Hope doubtless couldn't stand him now, and do what he had to do at the party to make it a success.

The room at the hotel was about a third of the size of the ballroom he'd used for the fund-raiser. He made a mental note to thank his office staff for the great job they'd done with the tinsel and garland draped everywhere. A few of the trees they'd used at the other party lit several corners, and various other Christmas decorations made it all look merry and festive for the guests.

Merry and festive. Not a chance he'd feel even a twinge of that.

He tried hard to get into party mode, smiling at several women dressed as elves, complete with pointy hats and curled slippers with bells, who were handing out small wrapped gifts to excited children. Other folks from the hospital were setting up games or already in the middle of one, and more volunteers were unveiling cupcakes and fruits and other treats that had been placed on a long table covered by a cheerful red tablecloth.

What he didn't see anywhere was Hope Sanders.

Could she have decided not to come? He sure couldn't blame her if she had.

He scanned the room again, and to his shock realized the tightness in his chest wasn't about hating to see disgust or dislike or anger in Hope's eyes. Or some kind of weird manifestation of relief that he apparently didn't have to face it. The squeezing sensation that made it a little hard to breathe was instead a deep and heavy disappointment that she hadn't come.

And how messed up was that? Despite everything, he'd wanted to look at her, talk with her, spend just a little more time with her, no matter if he stood on the lowest rung of her opinion now or not.

Then a flash of golden hair caught his peripheral vision, and he turned, hardly believing it was her emerging from behind one of the Christmas trees with a ball in her hand, holding it up with a beautiful smile on her sweet face. "Here it is! Hiding!"

"Thanks, Miss Hope! I can't believe it rolled all the way back there," a little girl said, giggling as she took the ball and ran back to whatever game she'd been playing.

The hard thump in his chest seemed to obliterate that nasty, squeezing sensation, and he found himself walking toward her before he'd even thought about what he could say. Should say. Or even if he should approach her at all.

But before he got close she was swept away by some other children to play what looked like musical chairs. A game like that wasn't his thing, so he decided to just stand back and watch her. To enjoy the way the light caught in her hair, making it gleam. To see her enthusiasm and laughter and the patient way she explained the game to those who didn't know it. To take in the heartfelt hugs she gave the children when they won or lost, encouraging them to try again.

He shook his head, upset with himself all over again. How could he have thought for one second this woman might struggle with having children on her own? No matter his own dark history, he should have realized that warm, sweet, upbeat Hope Sanders had plenty of resilience, love and caring to handle it.

With a toddler propped on her hip, Hope headed toward the snack table and handed the child over to a smiling auburn-haired woman he was pretty sure was a midwife new to the CRMU. As Hope turned back to the game their eyes met across the room. She stood very still for a moment, and Aaron's heart about stopped with her. His brain spun through the ways he might approach starting a conversation.

A conversation and an apology.

But before he came up with anything that felt right, that he thought Hope might be willing to hear, she'd begun to move across the room. His heart started back up again, thumping hard with every step she took, and he couldn't take his eyes off the way her skirt swayed gently on her slim hips. The way her hair, too, moved with the same rhythm and suddenly he was struck right between the eyes with another bizarre and awkward revelation.

He felt jealous of the damned anonymous sperm donor that would father Hope's children.

Crazy, idiotic and ridiculous, yes, but he couldn't deny that emotion, stunning though it was. Couldn't pretend it hadn't been part of the reason he'd been unable to keep his opinion to himself instead of confronting and lecturing her.

Which maybe meant he should schedule an appointment with a damned shrink.

He'd never wanted to be committed to one place or one person, and sure as hell had no idea what it took to be a father. Yes, his adoptive dad had been a good role model, though Aaron hadn't been able to see or appreciate that for a long time. But his sperm-donor biological father? He'd gotten half of his genes from that man and didn't want to think about the kind of person he might have been. And the genes from his poor, unstable biological mother?

Not something he wanted to pass on to any child.

But that kind of introspection was disturbing, unwelcome and pointless. He moved to talk to some of the party guests, shoving it all aside, trying very hard to concentrate on everyone he was speaking with and not looking at Hope. But when he did, she seemed clearly focused on a similar goal of not looking at him.

"Nice party you've got here," one of the adoptive dads said to him as they stood by a table of children and adults enjoying the various snacks together. "My wife and I have met quite a few kids the past few months, but this has been hands-down the best environment to talk with them and see them in action. They're a lot more relaxed, you know? And I guess we are, too."

Aaron smiled. "That's the goal, so I'm glad to hear it. Have you—"

The sound of a metal chair toppling over with a clatter interrupted him. He glanced over to see a boy, probably about six years old, pretty much underneath it and kind of rolling around on the floor.

A woman sitting next to the toppled chair shook her head and grinned. "I think that's the fourth boy who's tripped over a chair to get some attention. Guess they don't need to play a game to be silly."

But the blood-curdling shriek that came from the child instantly wiped the humor from everyone's face. Aaron quickly strode over and pulled the chair off the child, setting it upright, and adrenaline rushed through his veins at what was more than obvious.

CHAPTER TEN

AARON CROUCHED DOWN, putting his hands on the boy to try to keep him from writhing around so much and hurting himself worse. "It's all right. You're going to be fine. I'm Dr. Cartwright. Take a breath and tell me where it hurts."

The boy stared up at him with tearful, terrified eyes. "It's my arm. It hurts. My arm hurts."

"I thought so. Let me see if I can help." He turned to the crowd gathering around. "Someone call the emergency squad. Everybody back off, please, so he can breathe."

He gently put his fingers on the child's arm, gritting his teeth at the shriek his barest touch had elicited. Even if he hadn't been a medical professional, he'd have known the kid's arm was broken pretty badly. His forearm was curved at such an odd angle a compound fracture was likely, but thankfully the bone hadn't torn through the skin.

"Oh, my heavens, Aaron, what happened?"

He glanced up to see Hope's worried face just before she crouched down next to him. He hadn't said anything to the boy yet, so he addressed him first, hoping to keep him from getting more scared. "Looks like you've probably got a broken arm, buddy. We're going to have to take you to a hospital to get it fixed up. How do you feel?"

"It hurts. I feel…sick."

He glanced at Hope, who leaped up to grab a small trash pail, just in case. Aaron pressed his fingers to the wrist of the child's uninjured arm to check his pulse as Hope crouched next to him again.

"He looks clammy," she said in a near whisper.

"Yeah. His pulse is a little thready, too." They didn't want the boy fainting on them or going into shock, and he turned to the child again. "We're going to get you a little more comfortable, okay?" He raised his voice to the crowd. "Can somebody find us a tablecloth, or a few coats? And I need one or two of those cupcake boxes emptied and brought over here, and some sturdy twine or a rag I can tear into strips."

Numerous adults sprang into action, and in no time several coats were dropped onto the floor by their feet. Obviously knowing why he'd asked for them, Hope quickly folded the coats as Aaron tried to barely move the boy into position, doing it as gently as possible. Just enough to get his feet up, being careful to not jostle the broken bone. The child cried out and moaned again, clutching his arm close to his body.

Damn. "Try not to move your hurt arm at all, okay?" The boy nodded, but Aaron knew that might be difficult for him and decided he had to get it stabilized fast to make sure he didn't. Last thing the kid needed was to move in such a way that the bone broke through the skin.

"Anybody able to get those cupcake boxes to me?"

"Working on it," someone answered.

Hope slid the jackets under the boy's feet before he'd had to ask her to, then placed a folded tablecloth under his head to keep it from pressing on the hard floor.

"Better, buddy?" he asked the boy, glad that he nodded in answer.

"His name's Ethan," a woman's tremulous voice said.

"Ethan." He patted the child's chest. "You're doing a good job staying still, Ethan."

"I'm trying. But it hurts so much."

"I know. I'm sorry it hurts." He took the kid's good hand and pinched the nail bed of several fingers.

"Checking his capillary refill?" Hope asked.

"Yes. Want to make sure the break hasn't impinged on his arteries. But the nail bed's pinking back up nicely, so it doesn't look like that's happened."

"Good." Hope clasped the boy's hand after Aaron let go of the child's fingers. "You're being so brave, Ethan. Hang in there just a little while longer, okay? The ambulance will be here soon."

Aaron marveled at her soothing and reassuring tone. So reassuring, the boy actually managed to give her a wan smile in return. The warm, sweet smile she sent back, the way she held his hand gently between both of hers, would make anybody feel better. CRMU was damned lucky to have this woman as a nurse and midwife, and so were her patients.

And he'd been lucky to get to spend even one day with her. Which made him want to kick himself all over again that he'd lost control and said things he shouldn't have.

Reassured a little though he seemed to be, the child's worried brown eyes kept moving from Hope to Aaron and back again. He'd fidget then cry out in pain, but in another minute he'd be fidgeting again. Injury or not, expecting a young child to stay completely still was probably asking the impossible, and Aaron knew he had to get the arm stabilized fast.

The EMTs would have the right equipment, and he wished he could wait for them to get there. But all it might take to damage the arm worse would be for the boy to slide it down his belly or clutch it to his chest.

"Is this how you want the empty boxes?" a man asked, holding them out. "Or is there something else you need me to do with them?"

"We'll take them just like that," Aaron said. "Thanks. We'll need that twine, too, or rags. Anybody find something like that?"

"I'm on it," the man said.

Aaron set the boxes on the floor and Hope's eyes met his. "Are you planning to use those as a splint?"

"You're one smart woman, you know that?" He had to believe not many people would have realized that, including plenty of doctors and nurses.

"I know." Her lips curved. "How do you want to do this?"

"That's the tricky part. I don't know exactly, because obviously I'm trying to avoid moving his arm and don't want trying to splint it to end up making it worse instead of better." The boy was looking more scared again, and he gave him a smile. "We want to splint your arm, using a kind of field medicine, like soldiers might do. Maybe you can pretend you're in the army and you've got a battle wound we have to fix up."

"I don't want to be in the army," the boy said, his lip quivering as tears filled his eyes again.

Well, damn. That strategy hadn't worked too well. Aaron looked to Hope. Maybe she had a better idea.

"What kinds of toys do you like to play with?" she asked.

"I don't know." Ethan sniffed back the tears. "Dinosaurs. Cars."

"Do you play with those cars that transform into giant robots? Maybe when we put the splint on your arm, we can pretend you're a car that's out of gas and can't move and the bad guys are after you. But after the splint's on, you'll transform into the giant robot to fight off the bad guys."

"O...Okay." He gave her a smile and looked a little starstruck.

Aaron figured that was probably the way he always looked at Hope, too. He leaned close to her ear. "Did I say smart? Brilliant's more like it."

"You're just now realizing this?"

"As you've already learned, I'm not too bright." Her eyes were on his again, and he hoped she knew what he was saying. Giving her an apology before he was able to apologize for real.

"Got this from the hotel," the helpful man said, handing him what looked like thick kitchen twine.

"This is perfect. Thank you. Robot time, Ethan. Remember, you can't move at all until I've transformed you, okay?" He turned to Hope. "I'm going to slide the cardboard under his arm, and with any luck I'll barely move it from where it's resting on his belly. Why don't you try to gently hold his arm as steady as possible while I do?"

She nodded. "Got it."

Hope held Ethan's hand with hers, and cupped

the boy's elbow with her other hand. Aaron carefully slid the cardboard between his arm and stomach, glad the child wasn't shrieking again, just giving the occasional little gasp of pain. "You're doing great, Ethan. Only a little more and I'll have it all the way under your arm."

Sweating a little now, Aaron finally got it in place, sucking in a relieved breath. "Okay. I'm going to fold this sort of tube around his arm and you tie it in place, Hope."

"Already have some pieces cut. I hope they're the right size."

He held the cardboard curved around the boy's arm and watched Hope tie it on with the string loops about an inch apart. As he watched her work he found himself looking at her, the picture of avid concentration. Her lashes were lowered, as she watched herself work. Her brows were knit, and her white teeth sank into her bottom lip.

He could look at her for hours and never tire of the view.

"That's it, I think. Have a look, Dr. Cartwright."

"Perfect." He turned to smile at the boy. "Your transformation is complete, Ethan."

"You know, if you weren't a robot, I'd say you

look an awful lot like a trussed roast, Ethan," Hope said with a grin, giving his nose a gentle flick.

The child actually managed a little laugh. "A roasted robot, that's what I am."

Hope looked at Aaron as their eyes met and held, and they both chuckled. The woman was downright magical with kids.

And to think that instead of admiring that about her, he'd insulted her, saying she might not be able to handle being a single mother.

What a damned idiot.

Just as Aaron was trying to figure out what to say or do next the EMTs came in with a cart and equipment.

"Well, you've battled off the bad guys, and now the good guys have arrived, Ethan," he said. "They're going to get you all fixed up and take good care of you, okay?" Ethan nodded, and Aaron stood, reaching for Hope's hand to help her to her feet. They moved out of the way to give the emergency medical team a chance to work, checking Ethan's vital signs and getting him ready to transfer.

He studied Hope's elegant profile as she watched

the EMTs, trying to decide if he should dive into his apology right then, in case he didn't have a chance later. But first, he had to make a point of something else. "You were great with Ethan tonight, Hope. Don't know what I would have done without you."

"You were wonderful, too, Aaron. And all the others who helped, as well. I guess it took a bit of a village, didn't it?" She waved her hand around the room, and he captured it in his again, because he wanted to hold it. Wanted to see if she'd pull it away. Realized, when she didn't, that he'd never in his life cared so much about something as simple as holding a woman's hand.

"I have a feeling if not another soul had been here, you would have done just fine all by yourself." In fact, he was sure that statement was absolutely true. The woman was softness and steel. A gentle nurse and a fearless warrior. He drew her closer, and, when she didn't step back or pull away, the discomfort he'd been feeling since their last, ill-fated meeting eased just a little. He leaned closer. "Can it be our secret again that I haven't seen a broken arm since med school?"

"No. Makes you all the more heroic." She cutely

tilted her head. "Just think. When the story hits the local papers about this happening at the wonderful party designed to help children find parents, and the founder of the program who happens to be an OB managed to help a child with a seriously broken arm, people will be impressed. And donations will pour in. The end."

"Well, if that's the angle, I guess I have to go along with it." He had to grin. "What did I say before about you being a PR genius?"

"Did you say that? I don't remember." The way her kissable mouth and beautiful eyes were smiling at him took away a few more of the bruises from the self-bashing he'd given himself after lambasting her, and that he well deserved. "But I do remember other things you said to me just recently that were not so nice."

Her smile completely disappeared and her eyes got all serious. Damn it. But who could blame her? Calling his words "not nice" was an understatement. Seeing the change in her brought the ache about what he'd said surging back into his chest, but that wasn't important. What was important was that he'd hurt *her.* Had shocked and wounded her with his autocratic attitude and judgment, and now was the time to tell her how bad he felt about it. "Listen, I—"

"Is there a parent or guardian who can sign for the patient? And who wants to come to the hospital with us?"

Aaron realized the social worker who had brought a number of children to the party was looking to him with a question in her eyes. Damn. He hesitated for a split second, then gave her a quick nod before he turned back to Hope. "I really need to talk with you, but I have to take care of this first. Can I call you later?"

"All right." Her eyes were still oh-so-serious when he turned to the EMTs.

Aaron wished like hell he could apologize and somehow try to explain a little to Hope right now, but this had to be his top priority. "I'll come." He looked at the social worker. "I know you have to stay here with the other kids and get them back after the party's over. I'll take care of Ethan and keep you posted on whether or not they want to keep him overnight."

"I'm sorry this had to happen to take you from the party, but the rest of the children are having a lot of fun," she said.

"It's fine." He stepped to the gurney and placed his hand on the boy's leg, giving him a smile, hoping he felt at least a little reassured. "I'm coming with you to the hospital. The doctors and nurses will take good care of you, and I will, too, until we can get hold of your foster parents. Okay?"

Ethan nodded, looking grave but thankfully not too afraid. Aaron turned to look at Hope, glad to see she was still standing there. He couldn't tell exactly what expression was on her face, but at least it seemed she wasn't furious with him anymore. He gave her a twisted smile, hoping she'd interpret it the way he wanted her to. Which was that he knew he'd been an ass and owed her an apology.

He turned to the EMTs. "I'll sign everything on the way."

"Wait!" A woman rushed toward them with a man following behind. "Wait, please. We want to come to the hospital with Ethan. To...to get to know him better." She reached for the child's hand with a tender smile, and Aaron was surprised but happy to see Ethan smile back. "Would that be okay with you, Ethan?"

The boy nodded, still smiling, and the man

turned to Aaron. "Would we be allowed to do that? We're very interested in spending more time with him now and over Christmas and all."

Well, how about that? Maybe Ethan's mishap would end up being a good thing in the end, giving them all more time to spend together. "Looks like he'd like that. I'll have to sign the medical release papers, and one of the social workers will catch up with you at the hospital to make various arrangements, but otherwise it sounds like a good plan."

With the paperwork signed and Ethan and crew gone, the party resumed, slightly subdued but still festive and fun for the kids. People kept coming up to talk to him and pump his hand, and, while their praise felt a little uncomfortable, maybe Hope was right. Maybe an unfortunate event like Ethan's could turn out to be a good thing. The child might have a new family, and the foundation might get some new donors.

Between conversations, Aaron's attention kept going straight to Hope. To see her sitting at a table with rambunctious children, smashing and squeezing modeling clay to make some kind of creatures. Laughing as she dove toward a chair when the music stopped, pretending to get bumped out of it by a giggling child. Helping little ones, too small to reach everything on the table, fill their plates with goodies.

Accomplished at her job, great with kids, warm, stable, caring and beautiful beyond belief—was there a woman on the planet more perfect than Hope Sanders?

He turned to shake hands with someone else who'd approached him, wondering why thinking about Hope and how amazing she was brought a stab of something uncomfortable to his chest. Probably because he hadn't had the chance to say he was sorry.

Past time for that to happen, and when he was done with his conversation he scanned the room. His gut tightened when he didn't see her. Surely she hadn't left without saying goodbye? Then again, just because they'd helped little Ethan together didn't mean she had any interest in further interaction.

It was clear she was no longer around all the games the children were playing. He had to talk to her. Had to apologize. If she'd just left, maybe he could still catch her in the parking lot. He was about to ask one of the midwives accompanying Hope, but he somehow felt her presence a moment before her golden hair appeared at his shoulder.

Mussed golden hair, with glitter sparkling in it he didn't think was an intentional festive accessory. "All partied out?" he asked, feeling stupidly happy that she was still here, and wondering how any woman could look sweet and adorable and sinfully sexy all at the same time.

"It's been exhausting, I admit, but fun. How about you?"

"Definitely partied out." He grasped a strand of her hair and slid his thumb and forefinger slowly down it. "I like the fashion statement. Though I wouldn't have thought you were a glitter kind of girl."

She laughed softly. "Maybe you don't know the real me."

"Maybe I don't." Which was a good segue to his overdue apology. Except he hated to see the relaxed, happy look she was giving him turn into anger, disgust or dislike or whatever she'd been feeling toward him before tonight. He steeled himself, knowing he had to take whatever lumps were coming regardless. "Hope, I want to apologize for all the things I said to you about your IVF plans. How upset I got about it. I have no right to judge you or lecture you. I was totally out of line."

"Yes, you were."

He waited silently, thinking there must be more coming, like her berating him right back. But she just kept looking at him, and for once her face didn't reveal anything of what she was thinking or feeling. "So." His planned-out apology and explanation seemed to have disappeared from his brain, leaving him floundering a little. "I hope you'll accept my apology. I've seen how smart and competent you are at your job, and now I've seen how great you are with children. If you're sure IVF is what you want, I wish you the best of luck."

He still felt pinned by that blue, impassive gaze of hers and started sweating almost as much as he had getting Ethan's splint on. "You know, you're making me nervous," he said. "Is this your payback for me being rude? You aren't rude back, just an expert at making people feel uncomfortable?"

"I don't try to make people feel uncomfortable. Maybe there's some other reason you do. Maybe it's because you owe me a little more of an explanation for why you went off on me like you did."

Maybe he did. But he wasn't going to go there. "I've just seen a lot of families, and particularly single parents, struggle with multiple births and the problems that can come with that. Preterm and low-birthweight babies, and infants with birth defects, all of which have special needs on top of the normal stress of parenting multiples. That's all. But I know you feel you have support and you're prepared, and I apologize again for saying otherwise."

Those blue eyes still seemed to be looking right through him, seeing things he didn't want her to see, when she finally spoke. "You want to come to the Mill Road Winter Fair with me this weekend?"

He blinked. Of all the things she might possibly have said just then, inviting him on a date wouldn't have crossed his mind as one of them. He wanted to shout, *Hell, yes,* but had to wonder why she'd asked. "Aren't you the woman who said our fling was over and done with?"

"It is. But now you know why, which also

means you understand and accept that we're just friends. Plus I have an ulterior motive."

"I'm guessing this could be some kind of payback for my being unpleasant to you?" Her eyes were gleaming with mischief, and he wondered what she had up her sleeve.

"You would guess right. I'm volunteering at one of the food stalls selling smoothies. Proceeds go to a literacy foundation, and we're shorthanded. Seeing you do emergency surgery the other day tells me you'll be excellent at cutting various fruits to make the smoothies."

That surprised a laugh out of him. The little smirk on her face told him she knew full well he couldn't say no, that he owed her after his prior idiocy. Funny thing was, standing in some food stall all day slicing fruit with her somehow sounded pretty good to him, just as friends or more than that.

More than that couldn't happen now anyway, though, remember? Even if she wasn't planning on IVF, she was obviously a woman who wanted a forever after with kids and a homestead with a picket fence, and he just wasn't that kind of guy.

Being just friends, though? He wasn't sure he

could handle that, either, since his thoughts turned to kissing that beautiful mouth and touching her soft skin every time he was anywhere near her. Had to admit, too, that being friends with her while she was pregnant probably would be difficult for him to deal with for all kinds of reasons. Not the least of which had been the extent of his surprising reaction, and his complete inability to control it, when he'd first learned her baby plans.

Her blue eyes were looking at him expectantly, and the smile in them had him feeling good for the first time all day. And that feeling had him wanting to join Hope for one more, no-strings-attached encounter before she moved on with her life, even though it was a bad idea.

"Slicing fruit with you sounds like the best offer I've had all week."

CHAPTER ELEVEN

HOPE DUMPED WHAT seemed like the hundredth batch of cut fruit into the electric blender to join the yogurt, milk and juice and gave it good long zap before pouring it into a cup. "A Mill Road smoothie, made just for you," she said, handing it to the young man who'd ordered it.

"That sounds like an advertising slogan," Aaron said, standing next to her chopping away as he had been for two hours without a complaint. She'd never have guessed when she'd admired him from afar at the hospital how multifaceted the man was, chopping fruit like a trained chef. Devoting all kinds of time to charity causes. "I still think you're fibbing about not moonlighting in the advertising business when you're not working at the hospital."

"Ah, you have no idea what I moonlight at. Maybe I'm a punt-boat operator." She sent him a glance meant to be teasing, since he knew from experience she was not at all adept at punting.

But the brown eyes that met hers weren't laughing, they were...heated? Maybe even hungry, but not in a let's-eat-some-of-this-fruit kind of way. Instantly, she realized her words had sent his mind back to their time on the punt, to all that kissing and touching and maybe even to what came after they were back on dry land, snug in his apartment.

And then her mind went there as well, which made her notice all over again the width of his shoulders, the rippling muscles in his forearms as he chopped, the handsome planes of his face. How he looked far more deliciously edible than any fruit ever could.

He leaned close, his lips inches from her cheek. "If the moonlighting punt-boat operator doesn't stop looking at me like that, I might have to pull you into my arms and kiss you, forgetting we're just friends and that I have fruit and juice all over my hands." His voice was low and sexy, and the eyes meeting hers shined dark and hot.

"I'm not looking at you any way, except to wonder why you're so slow at chopping," she said, quickly turning her face to dump more stuff in the blender. "Don't you see the line we have here?"

"Mmm-hmm. If you say so."

Okay, it was true, darn it. Her heart had fluttered and her breathing went a little haywire just from admiring him. The question was, why? Yes, they'd steamed up the sheets together, which had been admittedly very, very nice. Incredible, really.

But what about the fact that he'd been an insulting jerk, too? His words still stung if she let herself think about them, and the only reason she'd invited him to join her today was because she'd realized at the party that, unbelievable as it seemed, he'd looked surprisingly vulnerable when he'd apologized for that.

Seeing that briefly unguarded moment had made her caregiving instincts jump up to step in. Could talented, confident Aaron Cartwright have something in his history, some kind of demon that haunted him? Something from his days in foster care that would be good for him to talk about?

Holding pain deep inside, refusing to share it, was hard on anyone, which was why she'd impulsively invited him here today. Thinking that perhaps spending time at the merry, entertaining atmosphere of the festival might relax him enough to unburden himself.

Only problem was, she'd thought his anger with her, and hers with him, would have smothered all that chemistry between them, leaving behind just a cordial friendship. Clearly she'd been utterly wrong, and how could that be, considering everything?

Somehow, she'd have to tamp it down when she tried to coax answers out of him. Then, whether he did or didn't talk about himself to her, this absolutely had to be their last day together as she started her new life.

The life he didn't approve of at all, which was odd as heck considering what he did for a living.

Remembering that helped cool the heat she'd been feeling a minute ago, and she concentrated on selling and making as many smoothies as possible. Finally, their shift was over, and none too soon, because her back was starting to ache and she figured his had to be, too.

"You've been a trouper, Aaron." She tugged at her apron strings as the next shift took over, then stopped to stare at Aaron's hands as he wiped them on a towel. "Oh, my gosh, your poor fingers are all pruney! I'm sorry—you should have asked to switch with me and let me take over the chopping for a while."

"I'd rather my hands get pruney than your pretty ones," he said. "Besides, I'm hoping that seeing me suffer like this for you will put me back in your good graces."

"You don't have to suffer to get back in my good graces," she said, surprised that, even though his lips were curved, his eyes looked serious. "You apologized and also helped here. Forgiven."

"Thank you. Not sure I deserve it, but I appreciate it." He lifted her apron over her head then smoothed back her hair, his gaze still on hers. "So what now? Do I have to cut up smelly fish for a couple more hours to make fish smoothies?"

"Oh, yuck. No!" A laugh bubbled from her throat. "I think you just might have ruined my appetite for the rest of the day." How had she not realized before what a good sense of humor he had? Maybe because she'd been noticing everything else about him. Like his good looks, and how wonderful it had felt to touch the softness of his skin over all those hard muscles of his. Sensuously shaped lips that had made her utterly mindless when he'd kissed her.

No. Not going to think about any of that ever again. "Let's just walk for a bit, see what we find to do," she said a little breathlessly. She moved into the flow of the crowd, trying to think of what he might enjoy, and when the time might be right to pry into his life to play therapist. Then had to stop for a second to bend to each side, trying to loosen her tight muscles. "How come my back hurts standing in one place for two hours, when it never hurts running around the hospital, even after a ten-hour shift?"

"Because when you're moving around the hospital, you're using all your back muscles. Standing still in one position too long strains the extensor muscles at the back of your spine that help you stand straight, making them feel stiff." His eyes were fixed on her body as she stretched, and his voice went lower. "I'd be happy to give you a back massage. I'm pretty good at it."

She'd bet he was. Also good at turning that back massage into something more, no doubt. "It was a rhetorical question, Dr. Cartwright. I did have to study anatomy, you know."

"I do know. And I liked it a lot when you studied my anatomy."

That wicked glint was back in his eyes and she folded her arms across her chest and glared at him in the hopes that he wouldn't know her thoughts had gone straight to his deliciously awesome anatomy, and that he made her want to laugh again. "Ground rules. Amusing though you are, the suggestive remarks need to stop. Just friends, remember? And for obvious reasons, after today we won't even be that."

"Sorry. Something about you makes me want to tease like a teenager, but I'll be good."

Yes, the darned man was good all right. Very, very good.

She cleared her throat. "So, what would you like to do? There are art exhibits and all kinds of musicians and bands here and there, which we'll see as we walk around. Lots of restaurants have foods out on the pavement, usually their specialties, and other food stalls like ours are everywhere, if you're hungry. And then there's dancing."

"I think I already told you moving from one foot to the other is about the extent of my dancing skills. But if there's dancing you like to watch, I'm good with that."

"Something you'd probably enjoy is the belly dancing. Might even want to give it a try."

He laughed. "Me belly dancing is such a horrifying visual I don't want to even think about it. But you?" He might have been talking about belly dancing, but his gaze was on her mouth, which sent her heart into that ridiculous pit-a-pat it kept doing around him, in spite of everything. "Seeing you belly dance would probably give me a heart attack."

"Wouldn't want that. But since it's not on my list of talents, nor do I keep a jewel in my belly button, I'm pretty sure your heart is safe."

He didn't answer, just stood there looking at her, oddly still and suddenly serious, as though she'd said something important instead of silly.

Then he turned away to scan the crowd of people, stuffing his hands into the pockets of his jeans. "What do you usually like to do here?"

The change from teasing camaraderie to the kind of slightly distant demeanor he would have engaged her with at the hospital before they'd met was a little unnerving. But him putting distance between them was a good thing, right? So she wouldn't have to.

As if she'd been doing a very good job of it anyway.

"Let's eat first. Smelling that fruit for so long made my stomach a little gurgly, wanting some real food."

"Anything but fish smoothies sounds good to me."

She laughed, relieved to see his normal teasing look was back, though why that seemed so important, she wasn't sure.

Both were silent as they made their way down streets crowded with all kinds of people, some dressed in period clothing, some wearing wild colors, their faces painted in bright blues, greens and reds, others wearing fairy wings and crazy hats and everything else imaginable. Aaron still hadn't spoken again, and she looked up at him, wondering what he thought of it all. The look on his face as he studied the crowd could only be described as dumbfounded, and she had to chuckle.

"Crazy, huh? And you haven't even seen what people dress up in for the parade."

"Do these people live in Cambridge?" he asked

in a tone that showed he found it hard to believe, and maybe a little alarming.

"A lot do. But plenty come from other places, even other countries. I think something like ten thousand people came to last year's festival."

"I'd always thought folks here seemed pretty normal."

"Don't be a fuddy-duddy. Dressing up and having fun is normal. Maybe you should try it." Though she had to admit she couldn't imagine it. The man practically exuded a level of testosterone that made it impossible to picture him in a silly costume.

"No, thanks. Unless wearing scrubs and pretending to be a doctor counts."

"Don't think it counts when you *are* a doctor, unless there's something you want to confess? Like you printed out your own medical degree from a six-week Internet course on fertility?"

"Ah, damn. You've found me out." His brown eyes twinkled at her. "Can we keep that just between the two of us? I need next week's paycheck."

"Our secret." She made an X across her heart. "You know, maybe being horrified by the idea of dressing up in a costume and having fun makes you the abnormal one," she joked, aware of a little happy feeling in her chest that they seemed to be back to enjoying the day the same way they had when they'd punted together, which was what she'd hoped for when she first suggested it.

Well, not exactly like that, since their boating trip had ended in lots of knee-melting kisses, not to mention a crashed boat and unforgettable love-making. Which she scolded herself for thinking of when he was standing right next to her, since he might see in her eyes exactly how those memories affected her.

"You know, I used to think I was pretty normal, but I'm beginning to wonder about that."

And there it was. That odd seriousness when he'd looked at her earlier. What was that about? Could it be a sign that the time was right to ask him more about his life, which she kept forgetting had been her ultimate goal for the day?

Just as she was pondering how to start that conversation, enticing scents from a grill set up outside a Middle Eastern restaurant wafted their way, apparently grabbing both their attention at the same time. Like tin soldiers winding down, they stopped mid-step, and the brown eyes that met hers were no longer serious but lit with anticipation.

"Are you feeling the same excitement my stomach is feeling? Because that smells incredibly good."

She pressed her palms to her suddenly growling belly, and blushed slightly at his chuckle, since he'd obviously heard. "Well, since we haven't come across any fish smoothies, we can settle for this, I guess."

"If we have to." He grinned at her, and insisted on paying as chicken kabobs and rice pilaf were piled onto paper plates and covered with some kind of thick yogurt sauce. Hope balanced the wobbly dish in her hands, wondering how she could manage to eat without spilling it all over her shirt, when one of the tables on the pavement was vacated at just the right moment.

"Come on." Aaron's long strides got there well before anyone else who'd been eyeing it could, and he set his plate down before pulling out a chair for her.

"This is perfect," she said. "Know why?"

"Because we don't have to balance our plates on one hand and eat standing up?"

"Because the parade will be coming down this street in about—" she glanced at her watch "—one minute. Believe me, you're going to be amazed at all the costumes and music."

Distant drumming, then accordion music and off-key singing drifted through the air, along with something that sounded like bells. Hope craned her neck, and, sure enough, dancers with outrageous costumes that looked like something from a bad outer-space movie appeared at the end of the street and headed their way as jesters hulahooped their way through the crowd in front of them. Behind the accordions, a tall, tree-shaped thing appeared, wrapped in a mishmash of fabrics with flags fluttering all over it. A woman stuck out of the top, a massive silver ball of something on her head, as the whole thing rolled down the street toward them.

Hope glanced at Aaron. He was holding his kabob stick between his thumb and forefinger, and it hung suspended in the air as he stared. His expression was so comical, she burst out laughing.

"I wondered why you'd invited me here after

you were mad at me for being so irritating." He turned that stunned look to her. "Now I know. You're torturing me for it. This is payback, isn't it?"

She nearly choked, laughing. "No. I swear. There really are a lot of fun things to do and see, and I find the costumes and silliness entertaining."

"You honestly like the costumes and…" he waved his kabob around "…all this?"

"I do." Maybe she should be irritated that he didn't get the Mill Road scene, but the almost little-boy bafflement on his face was adorable. "It didn't occur to me you'd be horrified. I thought you'd be amused. When we're done eating, we'll move on to other things you'll like. I promise."

"I'm not horrified. Just…confused." He lifted his free hand to her face and stroked a strand of hair from her eyes, his lips curving a little now. "But if you enjoy it, that's all that matters."

And wasn't that a sweet thing to say? His perplexed expression had melted away, and she could tell he really meant it. Her heart got a little squishy again, thinking about the giving, generous side of this man she'd already seen a number of times. Not at all like some of the doctors she'd worked with who were surprisingly arrogant, everything always having to revolve around what they wanted and how they wanted it.

It occurred to her that right then was the perfect time to talk to him. Instead of one-on-one with her where he might feel under a microscope, being in the middle of the crowd and loud performance seemed more casual somehow.

She set down her kabob, then hesitated, suddenly feeling doubtful about her plan. Probably because she didn't have any more right to ask him personal questions than he'd had lecturing her about her life. Could she just be being nosy? Just wanting to know more about super-sexy Aaron Cartwright and who he was before they didn't see each other again?

Maybe. But they were here now, and she might as well ask. If he didn't want to answer, he wouldn't.

She drew a breath then jumped in. "Can I ask you a personal question?"

The eyes that turned to her were instantly wary. "What kind of personal question?"

"I can't help but wonder why a fertility specialist would have such…surprising opinions about IVF and single women and multiple births. Isn't that all a part of what you do?"

He looked at her for a long moment before he spoke, his expression inscrutable. "I can't help but wonder why a beautiful woman, who any man would fall over himself to marry and have children with, wouldn't look for that instead of doing a procedure that leaves her with no help at home and her children without a father."

Her lips tightened. Here she'd wanted to have a conversation that might help him unburden himself about something, and instead it was leading right back to the argument they'd had before. "Any man? Pretty sure you said you were a man who wasn't interested in forever after, so does that mean there's something wrong with you?"

"Most men." A muscle ticked in his jaw as he modified that statement. "Not wanting that for myself doesn't mean there's something wrong with me."

"But me not wanting it for myself *does* mean there's something wrong with *me*?" Her heart slammed into her chest, because, yes, there might be something wrong with her, but since he didn't know that, his attitude was insulting. "A double standard for women and men? Wow, that's real fair, isn't it?"

"Never mind." He huffed out a breath and shook his head. "I don't want to get into another argument with you, and before I stick my foot in my mouth again, I'm shutting it."

"I already told you I'm apparently incapable of committing to a man. But I do want children, have always wanted children, and neither of those things means there's something wrong with me. But you know what is wrong with me?"

God, she was shaking. She sucked in a breath to control it, and tried to hold the words inside, just be quiet and get a grip on herself and walk away, but they burst out before she could stop them. "I have endometriosis. My parents had me when they were very young and insisted I not make the same mistake they did, having a baby before they were financially ready, then struggling to make ends meet. Things weren't good at home. Having a career before starting a family seemed best, that it would work for me. It never occurred to any of us that my mother being infertile from endometriosis in just her twenties might be genetic. But I'm thirty-four and, yeah, I have it. Does not being able to love a man, to want that kind of commitment in my life, destine me to be childless? I don't think it has to. And if I don't start a family now, it may be too late."

She jabbed her finger into his chest. "You don't want children, so you can't understand how I feel, how important it is to me. How I've pictured having a baby ever since I can remember. The truth? Yes, I'm scared I might not be a good mother. I'm afraid that my child will suffer not having a father, and that maybe it makes me selfish to have one anyway, just like you said. It worries me, but I'm trying hard to push that aside. To believe in myself and make my dream come true. And here you are, piling more weight on top of my fears." She dragged in a shaky breath. "No, you don't want children so you can't possibly understand my dream to have a baby that's mine. And since you don't understand, maybe don't even care to understand, you should keep your judgments and self-righteous opinions to yourself."

Unexpected tears stung her eyes and, horrified, she leaped from the chair and blindly made her way down the pavement, pushing her way through the crowd.

Where had all that come from? She swiped at her cheeks and kept going. Here she'd wanted him to unburden himself, and it ended up being her pouring her anxiety and pain all over him. Setting free all the emotion, the worry, the fear that had lodged deep inside after the failed artificial insemination attempts. Fear that she'd never have a child. Fears she hadn't even acknowledged—that maybe there really was something wrong with her that she couldn't say "yes" to George, that she was incapable of any kind of love. Fear that she'd be forever alone the rest of her life. With no one to love and care for. No one to love her in return.

"Hope! Hope, wait!"

She walked faster, not wanting to talk to him, to hear any more questions or criticism, to expose more of herself in such a public place.

"Hope, please stop."

A hand grasped her upper arm, effectively slowing her down. She tried to yank it loose, to no avail. His grip wasn't tight, but it was firm enough that she wasn't going anywhere, and he led her off the pavement, between two buildings and into the shadows.

"Hope, I'm sorry. I'm sorry." He turned her toward him and pulled her against his wide chest, his palm splayed on her back, holding her close. "I'm so sorry."

She stood stiffly in his arms, not wanting him to offer comfort. Not wanting to accept it. Not from a man who'd slammed her twice now for how she'd decided to live her life, and yes, she might be flawed as a woman, physically and emotionally flawed, but, if she was blessed enough to have the IVF work and have a beautiful baby that was all hers, she'd do everything in her power to be the kind of mother she wanted to be. The last thing she needed or wanted was for a man like Aaron to doubt that she could.

"Please let me go," she said, keeping her eyes level to stare at his coat button. "I'm going to get my bike and ride home."

"Hope." His big hand moved to her chin, lifting her gaze to his. It seemed there was shame in those brown eyes, a pain and remorse she thought she'd seen there before when he'd apologized, but it clearly meant nothing. It was lip service, nothing more, since he'd questioned her reasons, her choices, all over again. Probably, his "I'm sorry" were just words from a man who'd hoped to get her into bed one more time.

"Pretty sure we already had this conversation once. Let me go."

"Hope, please listen." His hand moved, gently cupping her cheek, and the intensity in his eyes pinned her with such fierceness she couldn't turn away from it. "I'm an idiot. A colossal one. I didn't have a right to question your choices before, and I sure as hell don't now. Instead of opening my big mouth the way I did, sounding like I disapproved all over again, I should have asked you to share with me how you're feeling about the IVF, if you're worried or if there was something I could help you with."

"I'm not worried about the IVF."

"No, but your medical condition worries you. And I'm sorry I upset you enough to tell me how hard this has been for you when you hadn't intended to share that. But while I am sorry, I'm also glad I know. I'm glad because, even though you might not believe it, I care about you." His hand slid across the side of her neck to tangle in her hair, cradling the back of her head, his eyes and voice softening as he drew her close. "That's really what this has all been about, even though I've shown it in a completely ass-backward way. I care about you and I can't help but worry about you, but because I'm a stupid man, I don't seem to be able to show that in the right way."

She stared into his eyes. Troubled, tender, full of that vulnerability she thought she'd seen before—all that emotion seemed to be right there in their brown depths. But she'd kidded herself about that before, hadn't she? She didn't know this man, not really, other than that he sometimes had a good sense of humor, was a great kisser and lovemaker, a caring person when it came to children without homes, and a great doctor.

And a man who didn't approve of single women having IVF, no matter what he was saying now.

Before she could pull away, his mouth lowered to hers, as soft and sweet as his words. Maybe it was because her emotions were already raw, or maybe it was because there was just something about him that reached inside her, touching her in good ways and bad. But she realized she didn't want to resist the kiss, to end it before it started, even though there were so many rea-sons she should. Her eyes drifted closed, and she gave herself up one last time to how he made her feel. Angry? Yes, that. But also wonderful. Deli-ciously aroused. Intoxicated with a kind of long-ing she'd never experienced in her life. A longing she'd believed she wasn't capable of.

His hands tightened, smashing her against his chest, and she clutched his shoulders and hung on. Let her fingers stroke his neck, slide up to curl into his thick soft hair, imprinting the feeling of every bit of it into her memory. Held his head still as she deepened the kiss, pulling a moan from his chest that seemed to reverberate through her own, shaking her heart. Until, somehow, she drew strength enough to separate her lips from his and pull away.

"So," he said, his voice rough, "is that a better way to show you, at least a little, how much I care about you? Help you forget all the wrong things I've said and forgive me?"

She tried for a light answer, something that would end the moment on a good note. A truce. Something that would close this brief time they'd spent together with a smile before the wave goodbye.

But she came up empty. As she let herself take in his features—his strong jaw, sensual lips, dark eyes she seemed to fall right into, all of the beautiful package that was Aaron Cartwright—the truth hit her like a blow to the solar plexus.

The tingle of her lips, the pounding of her heart, the way it felt perfectly right to be held close against his big body, were all proof that what she'd worried about for years was true.

There *was* something wrong with her. Really wrong. In all the years with George, in all the dates she'd experienced since, she'd never once felt the way she did with Aaron. Never had felt tempted to enjoy a fling the very first night she'd met someone. Never thought about a man all the time, never felt a heady, sexual pull every time he was near, never had a vision of a forever after that somehow felt absolutely right.

And the only time in her life she did? It was for a man who was a self-proclaimed rolling stone. A man who never stayed in one place very long, and who had zero interest in any kind of long-term relationship, especially a wife and children that would tie him down.

Was she the kind of woman only interested in a man she couldn't have? She'd never have dreamed that, but clearly she'd been deluding herself.

"I care about you, too. And while the things you've said hurt me, I figure some of it must come from your own pain. Your childhood in foster homes, even though you haven't said much about that. So I forgive you." She sucked in a fortifying breath, pressed her hands against his chest and took a firm step back, and the arms holding her close fell away. "Now we can close the chapter on our fling as friends. Thanks again for helping with the fruit. Goodbye, Aaron."

Somehow, she managed to put on a smile and stuck out her hand. Without returning her smile, Aaron looked at her hand for a long moment before he slowly engulfed it with his own. The smoky heat in his eyes faded to the seriousness she'd seen an awful lot of that day, and she found she couldn't look at it for another second.

She yanked her hand loose and practically ran out of the shadowy crevice they'd been standing in, praying he wouldn't follow her as she hurried the few blocks to her bicycle. But apparently he knew there was nothing else to say, because there was no voice behind her, calling her name this time. No hand grasping her arm to stop her.

Time to get her life back to its safe, steady track. Incomplete in many ways, yes, but hopefully a new addition would bring it closer to complete. Her heart and life would be filled to overflowing, which would be a very good thing, since right at that moment it felt all too sadly hollow.

CHAPTER TWELVE

"CONGRATULATIONS," AARON SAID, shaking the new father's hand. "Those are two beautiful baby girls you have there."

"Aren't they?" The man beamed. "Thank you for everything, Dr. Cartwright. We...we wouldn't have our daughters if not for you and can't tell you how much we appreciate it."

"Yes, thank you," the mother said with a smile overflowing in joy. "I'd shake your hand, too, except mine are a little full right now."

Aaron managed to smile back, but it was an effort. Looking at the blonde woman in the hospital bed, cradling a baby in each arm, made him think of Hope. Wonder about the babies she'd have, and if they'd favor her or their unknown sperm donor. Thinking how beautiful she'd look holding them in nine months if her own IVF treatment went well.

Her treatments that were about to start later that afternoon.

His gut tightened, feeling a little queasy, and he barely managed to eke out another smile as he gave his best wishes to the family and left the room, heading to his office for the rest of the day.

"What time is my first appointment?" he asked Sue, who was manning the front desk. He could have looked at the schedule himself, but didn't want to see Hope's name on Tom Devor's patient list.

Except he'd already snooped days ago. Maybe it verged on unethical, but he'd had to know. Then wished he hadn't looked, because the damned date had stuck in his brain, disturbingly nagging at him all week as it grew closer.

And now the day was here.

"One-fifteen," Sue said.

When she looked up at him, her smile turned to a small frown and he turned away. The woman seemed to have a sixth sense, and he sure as hell didn't need it boring into his brain today. "I'll be in my office."

He couldn't focus on paperwork and restlessly paced the room, finally stopping to stare out of the window at the heavy gray clouds in the over-cast December sky. He'd kept asking himself all week if there was something different he could have said to Hope, something that might have made her rethink her plans, and every time he wondered, he asked himself why.

His inappropriate criticism and his apologies to Hope, his sincere praise that she'd be a wonder-ful mother, were all utterly irrelevant to her life. What he thought or had to say didn't matter. She wanted a baby and didn't have a man in her life to give her one. IVF was a perfectly reasonable choice for someone like her who deserved chil-dren, and any children she had would deserve her. She'd been a short interlude in his life, and he in hers. Nothing more.

But it felt like more.

He had to get over it. Get over it, and be happy for her. It wasn't as though he could give her what she wanted, no matter how attracted they were to one another.

A soft knock at the door preceded Sue sticking her head in. "Mind if I come in?"

"Sure. What's up?"

"Your patient just called to say she's running

about ten minutes late." She stepped in and closed the door behind her, which Aaron took as a bad sign. "I can tell something's bothering you, and I'm guessing it's because Hope Sanders is starting her hormone treatments today."

Well, hell. He folded his arms across his chest. "Why would that bother me?"

"I don't know, you tell me." She mirrored his pose, standing there staring at him like a stern schoolmarm asking who threw the spitball.

Why *was* it bothering him so much? Good damned question, except he knew the answer. "Fine. I know you won't leave until I say something to make you leave. I like her. I'd like to date her, but she wants kids, and yeah, I guess that bothers me a little. But you know as well as anyone I'm not a home and hearth guy. In fact, I've been thinking it's time to move on."

As soon as he said it the idea again seemed painful and appealing at the same time. Not having to see Hope pregnant, not having to see her bring her babies to the hospital. Start fresh somewhere he would feel like his old self again.

"I charge my therapist fees by the minute so listen carefully." Sue stepped closer, resting her hand on his forearm, and the warm look in her eyes reminded him of his mother. His real one, who'd put up with so much from him. Not the crazy one he barely remembered. "You're a good man, Aaron. Maybe it's time you asked yourself why you move from place to place every few years. Why you avoid commitment like an infectious disease. Why the idea of a family of your own has you running the other way as fast as you can, when making families for others—for your patients and through your adoption foundation—is the one thing you *have* committed your life to."

"Helping people make families or become a family has nothing to do with my avoidance of one for myself," he said. Probably a damned lie, but he didn't feel like digging too deep into his psyche right then. "But I appreciate you caring about me enough to give advice."

Which was the reason he'd given to Hope for why he'd lectured her about having IVF as a single woman. Because he cared about her.

More than he could remember caring about any other woman.

"Just think about it," Sue said with another

pat on his arm. "I'll bring your patient when she gets here."

Being busy seeing patients the rest of the afternoon helped Aaron push thoughts of Hope to the side. He knew her appointment with Devor was scheduled at 4:00 p.m. and was glad he had a very nervous couple to talk to at that time, taking one hundred percent of his focus. After they'd left at four-thirty, he expected the knock at his door to be a nurse bringing his next patients in, leaving no time for anything but work.

Except it was Sue again, sans patients. "Your four-thirty canceled, and Dr. Krantz has some delay with the procedure he's doing. Would you mind talking to his patients for a few minutes? I've done what I can, but they're practically pacing a hole in the waiting room carpet. I'm thinking you can answer general questions to calm them down until Dr. Krantz can get here and take over."

"All right." Calming down nervous couples was something he thought he was fairly good at, and keeping busy was the goal. "You want to bring them in here, or to Krantz's office?"

"His, I think, so the patients can just stay there

when he takes over. How about I introduce you in the waiting room, and you can take them there?"

A horribly uncomfortable feeling swirled in his gut just like he'd felt earlier in the day as he followed Sue down the hall past Devor's closed office door. That it was happening again really started to tick him off, and just as he was welcoming some good self-disgust for being like some overemotional woman Devor's door swung open and out stumbled Hope.

And stumbled wasn't an overstatement. Two staggering steps, then her hand slapped against the doorjamb, hanging onto it like a lifeline. Her face was white as chalk, her eyes wide and a little glassy, and when they looked up and latched onto his she let out a short, distressed cry.

"Hope." He grabbed her arms to steady her. "Are you all right?"

"I...I..."

Damned if she didn't actually blanch even more, and her lips seemed to tremble when she stopped trying to talk. But her eyes, filled with something akin to panic, stayed focused on his. Had she somehow had some unusual, bad reaction to the hormones? It did happen sometimes, but never in his years of practice had he seen it occur that fast. He looked past her to Tom. "What happened?"

"She'll be fine." Tom's face was unreadable. "She needs to sit down for a few more minutes, that's all. Hope, come back in and catch your breath, okay?"

"No. I...I need to go home. I need to think."

Something about the way her eyes were fixed on his scared the hell out of Aaron, though he couldn't say exactly why. "Hope, listen," he said, having no clue what he wanted her to listen to. He just knew he had to somehow wipe whatever that was—shock maybe?—off her face.

"No. I have to go." She managed to pull out of Aaron's hold and, for a woman who'd looked as if she was going to faint just seconds ago, practically left skid marks on the floor as she left.

He wanted to chase after her, but he didn't have the right, damn it. Standing still and watching her leave took a Herculean effort, but she was Devor's patient. Sue managed the office; she was the one who took care of non-medical problems. And as for him?

He knew Hope didn't even count him as a friend anymore.

* * *

Hope wasn't sure exactly how she'd made it home, as it was a bit of a blur, but she was there, somehow, snug in her flannel pajamas. Or she would be snug, if her whole body didn't still feel icy cold from shock.

She scrubbed her cheeks with soap, hoping the everyday routine would bring a feeling of normalcy after every bit of it had gone straight out of the window an hour ago. Bring a little circulation back to her skin's current numbness as she tried to come to grips with this unbelievable reality.

A reality that felt totally unreal and impossible. A reality that in some ways was a dream come true. In other ways?

A total, unbelievable nightmare.

She toweled off her face then, like an automaton, walked into her living room. Slowly lowered herself onto the sofa to stare, unseeing, at the wall.

What in the world was she going to do?

Her hands went to her belly, instinctively. Protectively. And somehow, the simple movement calmed her.

The question her brain had asked in its panicked state wasn't the right one, was it? Obviously, without question, what she was going to do was have this baby she'd been blessed with. Not the way she'd planned, but things didn't always go to plan, did they?

She sat quietly, trying to process it, letting the truth of the situation seep through her body. Waited for the fear to jab at her again. The doubts that had plagued her as she'd tried to ready herself for the IVF and for having a baby.

But it didn't. Shock though it was, ideal situation though it wasn't, Hope found herself slowly filled with a quiet and deep gratitude. A warmth that spread through her being, chasing away her chill.

She was going to have a baby to love and care for and raise as best she could. Her dream, her wish, had been granted, and her heart suddenly bloomed with happiness, so full she thought it might burst right out of her chest with the joy of it all. Already being pregnant took all decisions out of the equation, didn't it? The questions of whether she should or shouldn't have IVF, be a single parent. Questions of whether or not she'd be able to love her baby the way it deserved to be loved.

The intense love already overflowing in her heart gave her that answer, and her throat closed with the relief of it, the joy of it.

So now, the only real question was, should she tell Aaron? Or let him assume she'd had the IVF procedure to get pregnant, and leave him out of their baby's life?

She closed her eyes and pictured the father of her baby. His handsome features, his teasing smile. His focused commitment to his patients, his caring for children.

Then there were his kisses. His touch. The way he made her feel like no one else ever had. Just thinking of it left her breathing shallow, made her heart flutter, made her long to hold him in her arms and have him hold her in return.

No. Oh, no. Her eyes flew open as she faced the incredible and terrifying truth.

She loved him. She was totally, absurdly, ridiculously in love with a man who didn't want that in his life. It wasn't some crazy thing where she just wanted a man she couldn't have.

No. She wasn't crazy. But she was crazy in love with Aaron.

She pressed her hands to her eyes, absorbing

the truth of how she felt. Knowing that, even if he shared some of her feelings, he didn't want a committed relationship. Didn't want a family. Didn't want to be tied down. Had openly stated it, and lived his life with that credo in mind.

How had this happened? How was it possible that all these years, from her teens into her thirties, she'd never experienced anything like this heady, wonderful, terrifying feeling? And because of that, had been so sure that George must have been right, that there was something fundamentally missing inside her. Whether it was her genes, her parents' lack of love for one another, who knew why, but she just wasn't capable of that kind of love.

Except she was. How she felt about Aaron proved that loud and clear.

Her hands slowly slid from her eyes, dropping into her lap. The irony was painful, yet thrilling, too.

She loved Aaron. The intense roller coaster of highs and lows these past weeks that had been knocking her all around, squeezing her chest and leaving her breathless, couldn't be mistaken for anything else.

Which meant she was fully capable of loving her baby the way she wanted to. Meant that maybe someday it was even possible she might love someone else, a man who wanted the same kind of life she did.

Aaron wasn't that man, and that knowledge painfully squeezed her heart. But he was a truly caring man—yes, he'd said some pretty awful things to her, but, as she'd guessed before, there just might be some reason for that, a reason he didn't share easily. Perhaps from his childhood, perhaps not, but everyone had issues, didn't they? She'd had plenty of her own.

Aaron's career and passion were about forming families, about bringing them together, and how wrong would it be to keep his own child a secret from him? Without giving him the chance, the opportunity, to decide if he wanted to be a part of his own child's life or not?

The calm fluttered, then settled right over her heart, and the answer was as clear as glass. He deserved to know, and their baby deserved it, too. He was a man who, even if he hadn't wanted it or planned for it, would take responsibility for his child and do everything he could to be a good father. She felt as sure of it as she was that the sun would rise tomorrow.

He probably couldn't love her the way she loved him, and that brought a heavy ache to the calm in her heart. But what was most important? That he love their child. And if somehow she was wrong, that he couldn't do that, offer that, she'd be back to where she'd expected to be all along. A single mother.

Except now she knew things would be just a little different from what she'd planned. She knew her heart would always carry an empty place that only Aaron could fill.

Last night, her plan had seemed so easy, so right. And when she'd called Aaron right after she'd made that plan, asking if he could meet her in his office at the end of the day, he'd sounded so normal, so much the caring Aaron with a warm concern in his voice, she'd convinced herself it would be okay. Difficult, yes, but okay.

Actually walking into his office at the end of the day to talk to him, though, was a different story. With her heart flying into a serious arrhythmia, creating a virtual timpani of anxiety in her chest, she thought she just might have to bail out and reschedule when she was calmer and more under control. When she might actually be able to breathe.

The office manager—Sue?—had greeted her, and something about the woman's expression upped Hope's anxiety even higher, wondering if she knew. But of course, even if she did, she couldn't know everything. Sue might know from Hope's file that she was already pregnant, but couldn't possibly know the father was Aaron.

Could she?

Lord. Hope wet her lips with her tongue and seriously contemplated running back out of the door. She stood, wiping her hands on her skirt, and just as she eyed her escape route Sue came over.

"Dr. Cartwright is ready to see you now."

"Oh. Okay. Thanks."

To her surprise, Sue gave her a big, warm smile and patted her on the back before leading her toward Aaron's office, nudging her inside. After a few, tentative steps, she stopped. Another smile from Sue helped her catch her breath and relax a smidge as the door clicked closed, leaving them alone.

In a very small room. That felt even smaller as she stared at Aaron's motionless back, and she nervously licked her lips. He stood looking out of the window, and his hands were clutching the back of his head, fingers entwined. Just as Hope was sucking in a calming breath and trying to rehearse what she was going to say, he turned.

And the expression on his face dried up every word on her tongue.

The man looked shaken. Pale. Staring at her as though he didn't know who or what he was looking at.

Oh, God. He knew. He already knew. And the shock and distress on his face told her loud and clear how he felt about it.

Also told her she'd been deluding herself bigtime. Ridiculously hoping, even if she hadn't admitted it to herself, that he'd be as excited as she was to be having a baby. How stupid could she have been, knowing how he'd always felt about being tied down?

Embarrassment, humiliation even, slid through her veins and left her frozen.

Aaron took two unsteady steps to his desk and pressed his palms to it, still staring at her with disbelief. "I just found out...I looked at your files. I know that...you...and...I can't believe it."

The man was nearly incoherent, and, while she'd expected him to be shocked, she hadn't expected this...this horror? To think she'd believed he'd accept it, take responsibility for their baby, be there to support her. She was such a pathetic fool.

"Obviously, you already know what I came to tell you." She hated that her voice was shaking instead of cool, as she'd wanted it to be. Hated that a deep, hidden part of her had secretly hoped he'd tell her he loved her, and their child, too, that this had somehow been meant to be all along, bringing the two of them together.

"Yes. But...my God, Hope."

Every shocked word seemed to stab another sharp nail into her already battered heart. "Don't worry yourself, Aaron. I'm... I'm sorry this happened. I know this isn't what either of us wanted or expected. As far as I'm concerned, the baby is mine and only mine. Simply what I'd planned on before...this. I just felt an obligation to tell you, but since you already know, I guess we're done here. Goodbye."

She turned on shaky legs to open the door, wanting out, wanting away from him and the look on his face that spelled out painfully clear that a child binding them together was the absolute last thing he'd ever want.

"Hope. Wait."

She looked back at him, and the utter loss and confusion in his gaze sliced at her again, leaving her bleeding. "It's fine, Aaron. You can keep your life of freedom. The last thing I would ever want is for you to feel tied down and obligated." As her own father had. "You know I'd planned to be a single mother. I don't need you or any other man to support me or to make me feel whole."

She made her way out of his office and through the main door, gulping back the tears, praying she didn't make any more of a fool of herself than she already had if he showed up in front of her.

Then realized the joke was on her again, because he hadn't followed her at all.

CHAPTER THIRTEEN

AARON'S OFFICE DOOR burst open without even a knock and a Sue Calloway he'd never seen before stalked to his desk and leaned forward, giving him a look that could only be described as the evil eye.

He'd probably have been shocked by it if he weren't numb from head to toe.

"What did you do to make Hope Sanders cry?"

That shook him out of his daze. "Cry?"

"Yes, cry. She came in here looking nervous and scared, and I was sure she'd leave looking calmer, relieved, maybe even happy, but no, she had big, fat tears streaming down her face. So what did you do?"

"Nothing." Which, since his senses were finally, slowly coming back to him, had doubtless been why Hope had blown in the door then right back out.

She'd come to tell him the unbelievable news,

and he'd barely been able to get a word out of his mouth, having finally gotten his hands on her chart just minutes before she showed up.

"I don't suppose you know who the father of her baby is," Sue said.

How the woman knew he couldn't imagine, but obviously that sixth sense of hers was in action. "I am. And I'm guessing that doesn't surprise you."

"Aaron." Her voice softened slightly. "From the second I saw the picture of you dancing with her, and the subtle changes in you since that day, good changes, I knew you were falling for her. I also was afraid you wouldn't let yourself."

It hadn't been a question of letting himself. He'd had no choice in the matter.

He loved her.

And he'd hurt her. Again. Let her down big-time at the exact wrong moment. But it hadn't been the shock of learning about the baby that had left him speechless. It had been the shock of real-izing exactly how much he loved her, needed her, wanted her in his life. Wanted their baby. For the forever after he'd never thought he'd want with anyone. Wouldn't ever be capable of with anyone.

And because that had been a lot of change for

his pitiful heart and brain to process, he'd stood there staring at her like a damn fool when she'd told him he could keep his life of freedom. A life he didn't want anymore. A life he now desperately wanted to replace with her and with their child.

He grabbed his coat, thankful his feet and mind were working again. "I need to go fix things with her, Sue."

She opened the door for him and gave him a wide smile. "You do that. Good luck."

He was damned glad he'd driven his car and not ridden his bike, and had to force himself to slow down before he got pulled over and delayed by a traffic ticket. Also needed to slow down because it was snowing, and skidding off the road wouldn't help get him to Hope so he could hold her and love her and beg her to forgive him. Again. For the third and most important time.

He ran up her snowy steps and banged on her door, his heart racing and his breath short. For the first time in his adult life, he was well and truly scared. He had no idea if Hope shared his feelings, if she wanted him in her and their baby's life, if she'd understand why he'd acted the way he had.

If she'd slam the door in his sorry face.

He banged on the door again, starting to panic that maybe she wasn't even home, that maybe she'd gone to her parents' house or something, and what would he do then? In mid-knock, it swung open, and he nearly dropped to his knees at the sight of her.

"Hope." He took in her tousled hair and her pink flannel pajamas, and she looked so sad and vulnerable it was all he could do not to sweep her up in his arms, but he knew she wouldn't welcome that after the way he'd acted. Her red-rimmed eyes and the single tear trickling down her cheek clutched at his heart, and he let himself at least reach to gently wipe it away, her cheek warm against his cold thumb. "Please let me come in. I have things I want to say to you."

"Do you?" He could see her deciding and he held his breath, praying she'd let him in and not force him to take the door off the hinges. "Funny, you didn't have much to say earlier."

"I know. And I'd like to explain why. Please."

"I know why. You don't w…want a baby to tie

you down." She sniffed and swiped at another trickle of tears. "I already told you not to worry. We'll be fine without you."

"But I won't be fine without *you*. And not wanting to be tied down isn't why I couldn't speak when you came into my office."

She didn't budge. He shook the snow from his head and tried another tack. "Even though you have every right to be upset with me, I know a caring nurse like you wouldn't want me to get hypothermia from spending the night out here, which I'll do if you don't let me in. Plus, a midwife letting her baby's father die on her front porch wouldn't be good PR for CRMU."

The tiniest curve of her lips and shake of her head had him holding his breath until she opened the door wider and stepped back. She didn't say a word, just walked toward her sofa, and he wanted to grab her up and kiss her and beg her to love him but knew there were things she had to hear from him first.

She gestured to her armchair, then sat stiffly on her sofa across from it. He pondered taking off his snowy coat, but worried she might think he was making himself a little too comfortable under the circumstances, so he sat. Their eyes met, and his nerves jangled all over again, because so much was riding on his words, and he'd done a damned poor job of expressing himself too many times the past weeks.

"When you came to my office, I'd just snooped into your file and found out you were pregnant. I'm sorry if that makes you mad, but I was worried about you."

"No need to be worried."

Her expression had cooled, and her eyes were starting to look a little hard, like blue ice, and he knew he'd better get it all said fast before she threw him out into the snow again. "I was stunned to hear about the baby, just as I'm sure you were, too. But that wasn't what shocked me. What shocked me was that, the second I read those words, I knew I loved you, Hope. More than anything or anyone in my life. And it shocked me that I felt like…like I'd come home. I've never really belonged anywhere my whole life, had been sure I never would, and in that split second all those convictions got turned on their head and I was still trying to process it all when you walked in."

Her eyes were wide on him now, and he could tell she was trying to decide if she could believe him. If he was saying it just because he felt responsible, and he moved to sit next to her, reaching to hold her hands, needing that connection. "I'm obviously a little slow to figure things out, but I finally get it. I was attracted to you the second I saw you at the party. Hell, I was attracted just seeing you in the hallway at work. And as I got to spend time with you, I loved your sense of humor and adventure. How you care for others, and how damned good you are at your job. The taste and feel of you, but I wouldn't let myself even think about loving you. Wouldn't let it happen."

"Why?" she whispered, her eyes searching his. "And why do you say you are now? I don't want our baby to force you into thinking you have to feel something, or say you feel something that you don't."

"I admit the baby was what forced me to open my eyes and my heart." He didn't want to go into the rest of it, but she deserved to know. "Forced me to look at myself and my attitudes and how I've lived. Probably I should have seen a psychologist long ago, but I'd stuffed down my past and refused to consider that it still impacted me today."

"What past? Your adoption?"

"No." He shook his head. "I told you my biological mother was unstable. But I didn't tell you all of it. She was single, older and wanted a baby. Like you. She had IVF, ending up with triplets. Apparently without much help at home. I don't know anything about her mental-health history prior to that, but she suffered from postpartum psychosis that dragged on a long time. Children's services got involved, but eventually she completely lost it and tried to kill herself. Ended up in a mental hospital. My siblings and I lived in various different foster homes, and I have vague memories of foster parents taking me to visit my mother in the hospital."

"Oh, my God, Aaron." Her hands tightened on his. "Now I understand why you were so upset with me about my IVF plans."

"I shouldn't have projected that on you, Hope, and I'm sorry."

"So what about your siblings? Do you ever see them?"

He briefly closed his eyes to that pain. "My biological mother gave us up and opted out of any contact. Not too many adoptive families want multiples, and we were separated in closed adoptions. A while back, I tried to find out who and where they are now, but had no luck. So I have a brother and sister somewhere I'll never know."

"That's...terrible." Tenderness and sympathy filled her blue eyes. "What was your biological mother's name?"

"Her name?" He stared at her, wondering why in the world she'd asked.

"Yes. You always refer to her as your biological mother, which seems so cold and distant. Maybe you do that on purpose, like she wasn't really part of your life. But for better or worse she was, Aaron. So I'd like to know her name."

"Anne. Her name was Anne." Funny how saying it did make her seem more real somehow, and not just a shadowy memory he preferred to forget.

"Anne. That's a nice name." She squeezed his hand. "I'm so sorry you went through such difficult times. I see why you started your adoption foundation, but I have to be honest. I'm surprised you decided to become a fertility specialist, considering everything."

"I guess it was my way of helping people make informed decisions, and implant only two eggs to hopefully prevent the kind of overwhelm my mother experienced." He realized he hadn't gotten to the most important thing yet. "Hearing about our baby slammed me with a truth I'd refused to admit was a problem, Hope. A truth I finally had to overcome. That in spite of having loving parents, I ran from commitment, never let myself get close to a woman, because I didn't want to expose myself to abandonment or pain. Pathetic, but true."

"Not pathetic." She held his face between her warm palms. "Not many people have to go through what you did."

"Loving you has changed that. Changed me."

Tears sprang into her eyes, but she didn't speak, and that scared the hell out of him. But he kept going because he had to. "I love you, Hope. I love you and I love our child, and all I want is for us to be a family together forever." He touched his lips to hers, barely able to whisper the next words, afraid to hear her answer. "Will you marry me,

Hope? Not because we're going to have a baby, but because I love you in a way I never knew it was possible to love someone, and I know now that I'll never be complete without you. I don't know if you feel the same way but..."

He found he couldn't finish the sentence, just stared into her beautiful eyes and willed her to love him back. Which maybe worked, or maybe she really did, because she wrapped her arms around his neck and kissed him.

"I do love you, Aaron Cartwright. So much." Her voice wobbled and her eyes filled with tears again that, this time, looked like happy ones. "We've had the same problem, you know. Until I met you, I thought something was missing inside me. Now I know what was missing was you."

Well, damn. He swallowed down the lump that formed in his throat at her words and wrapped his arms around her, holding her tight. "When I first danced with you, I thought it was fate that the music started back up just at the right time. Guess it really was."

"Is it fate that your child is going to grow up in Cambridge, so you can teach him or her how to be punt captain extraordinaire?"

"Maybe it is. But you're going to get that title first." He moved his mouth to her cheek, smiling against its softness. "You haven't answered my question, though."

"Question?"

"The 'will you marry me' question. Might not be important to you, but it's damned important to me."

She pulled back an inch, and as he looked into the blue of her eyes his chest filled with emotion all over again. If she gave him the answer he wanted, he'd get to lose himself in them every single day.

"Of course I'll marry you. I'd have to be completely crazy not to marry the world's most wonderful man."

"Can't claim that title, I know," he said against her lips. "World's luckiest man, though? With you in my life, I have that title in the bag."

EPILOGUE

"You're at nine centimeters, Hope, maybe even a smidge more," her midwife, Bonnie, said with a smile. "Getting close. I'll be back in just a bit to check on you."

"Doing good, sweetheart," Aaron said, dropping a kiss on her forehead. "How's it feel being on the other side of the bed?"

"Painful." She squeezed her handsome husband's hand, still a little in disbelief that he was all hers. "Being pregnant has given me a whole new appreciation for mothers everywhere. Waddling like a duck is no fun, and neither is being round as a beach ball."

"But you're the most beautiful beach-ball-shaped duck in the universe."

His eyes crinkled at the corners, until his smile was instantly wiped from his face as a contraction hit her and she moaned.

"All right. You're all right. Breathe. Breathe again."

When it was over, she let her head drop back against the pillow, and, now that the pain had faded, Aaron's anxious expression nearly made her laugh. "You'd have made a terrible midwife, and it's a good thing you became a fertility specialist instead of a practicing obstetrician. This is a normal part of the process."

"I know. But that doesn't mean I can feel blasé about you hurting." He rested his big hand on her belly and the smile came back to his face. "There's another kick. Our rugby player wants out of there."

"Or our superstar girl football player."

"And punt-boat operator. Let's hope for your sake it's not born with a pole already in hand."

She had to laugh at that horrifying visual, until she had another contraction to get through.

"These seem to be coming really close together," Aaron said, that frown dipping even deeper between his brows. "I should go find Bonnie."

"I think we can give it a few more minutes," Hope said, panting, though she had to admit he was right. They were coming fast. "Distract me with some conversation."

"Well, I was going to wait until after the baby came, but I guess I'll tell you now. Your hard work sleuthing through the newly opened California adoption records finally hit pay dirt. The Michael Krieger you thought might be my brother? Believe it or not, he is. He emailed me today."

"Oh, Aaron, that's wonderful! I'm so thrilled for—" A powerful contraction cut off her words and breath, and this one lasted so long, she thought the baby just might pop right on out. "Aaron," she gasped when she could speak again. "I think you're right. I think it's time. I—" She couldn't control the long moan, and between gasping breaths stared up at her anxious husband. "I have to push. Be ready, in case she's not back in time."

The alarm on his face would have been comical if she hadn't been hurting and pushing, and she still managed to nearly laugh as she spoke between contractions. "Why...are you looking like that? You're an OB, not a lawyer, for heaven's sake. If...the baby comes, you can handle it."

"Right." He practically ran to the sink to wash his hands and snap on gloves before positioning himself between her legs. "All right. I'm ready. Give me another push, sweetheart."

She did, and when it was over made a mental note to be even more sympathetic to mothers giving birth, because it hurt a whole lot more than she'd expected.

"You're doing great. Wonderful. Another push."

"I take back…what I said about you not…being a good midwife," she gasped.

"Oh, my God, Hope, it's crowning! It's coming! Another big push. You're amazing. Wonderful. Our baby's almost here."

"Dear me!" Bonnie exclaimed as she ran into the room. "I'm so sorry! I never dreamed you'd go that quick…" She let Aaron continue rather than disrupting the birth, but checked Hope's vitals and hovered for when Aaron needed her.

"Oh, Aaron. Is it…?"

"Coming. Yes. One more big push, honey. I've…got it!"

To her astonishment, he really did. Their baby was actually in his hands, and he brought it wet and wriggling to lie on her chest. "It's a girl! A beautiful, gorgeous baby girl."

"Oh, Aaron. I can't believe it." She held her

daughter close and stared at her tiny face and body. She thought she'd been awed every time she'd delivered a child? There was no comparison to the instant, soul-drenching love filling her chest. The baby gave a lusty cry that made both of them laugh. "Does she seem…all right?"

"She looks perfect in every way." His long fingers gently stroked her cheek. "Just like her mother."

"Here, let me take the baby and get her cleaned up, then I'll take care of you, Hope."

Bonnie carried the baby to the warming bassinet as Aaron snapped off his gloves, taking Hope's hands in his. She tore her gaze from their tiny newborn to look up at her husband, and her heart squeezed even tighter when she saw the tears streaking down his cheeks.

"Aaron." She lifted her hand to his face and gently wiped them away. "We have our miracle. I love you so much."

"I love you more than I could ever say, Hope." He leaned down to press his lips to hers. "Having you in my life is my first miracle. Thank you for that, and for giving me this second miracle, too."

She brought his head down to hers for a long

kiss, and, when she pulled back, saw Bonnie standing there holding their swaddled blessing. "Who gets her first?"

"Aaron," Hope quickly said, wanting him to have that happiness. "He brought her into the world."

"And you did all the work the past nine months and today, but I'll take her anyway." His cheeks still damp, he grinned and reached for the baby, then perched on the side of the bed.

"She has your amazing blue eyes," he said softly.

"Most newborns have blue eyes."

"Not like these." He turned her a bit so Hope could see her, too, and she couldn't believe what a vivid blue they were already.

"Oh, my goodness, I guess you're right. Her hair is pretty dark, though." She ran her finger tenderly across her daughter's downy eyebrows and round cheek, still hardly believing she was really here. "So are you still good with the name we picked?"

His elated gaze stayed on their baby's tiny face. "Yes. Caroline Anne is a beautiful name. I know my mothers would have loved her every bit as much as both of us already do."

"Yes," Hope agreed, the love for her daughter practically bursting from her chest the way she'd always dreamed. "They would indeed."

* * * * *

MILLS & BOON®
Large Print Medical

June

Playboy Doc's Mistletoe Kiss	Tina Beckett
Her Doctor's Christmas Proposal	Louisa George
From Christmas to Forever?	Marion Lennox
A Mummy to Make Christmas	Susanne Hampton
Miracle Under the Mistletoe	Jennifer Taylor
His Christmas Bride-to-Be	Abigail Gordon

July

A Daddy for Baby Zoe?	Fiona Lowe
A Love Against All Odds	Emily Forbes
Her Playboy's Proposal	Kate Hardy
One Night...with Her Boss	Annie O'Neil
A Mother for His Adopted Son	Lynne Marshall
A Kiss to Change Her Life	Karin Baine

August

His Shock Valentine's Proposal	Amy Ruttan
Craving Her Ex-Army Doc	Amy Ruttan
The Man She Could Never Forget	Meredith Webber
The Nurse Who Stole His Heart	Alison Roberts
Her Holiday Miracle	Joanna Neil
Discovering Dr Riley	Annie Claydon

MILLS & BOON®
Large Print Medical

September

The Socialite's Secret
London's Most Eligible Doctor
Saving Maddie's Baby
A Sheikh to Capture Her Heart
Breaking All Their Rules
One Life-Changing Night

Carol Marinelli
Annie O'Neil
Marion Lennox
Meredith Webber
Sue MacKay
Louisa Heaton

October

Seduced by the Heart Surgeon
Falling for the Single Dad
The Fling That Changed Everything
A Child to Open Their Hearts
The Greek Doctor's Secret Son
Caught in a Storm of Passion

Carol Marinelli
Emily Forbes
Alison Roberts
Marion Lennox
Jennifer Taylor
Lucy Ryder

November

Tempted by Hollywood's Top Doc
Perfect Rivals...
English Rose in the Outback
A Family for Chloe
The Doctor's Baby Secret
Married for the Boss's Baby

Louisa George
Amy Ruttan
Lucy Clark
Lucy Clark
Scarlet Wilson
Susan Carlisle